Whirligigs
For
Woodcarvers

Julie,
Thanks for an excellent
job of proof reading.
Have fun with whirlgigs.

Mike

Whirligigs
For
Woodcarvers

Michael P. O'Neil

All drawings, photographs, whirligigs
& woodcarvings by the author.

M & *M* Arts

Plainville Massachusetts

Copyright

Published by M and M Arts, 67 Spring Street, Plainville, MA 02762 www.mandmarts.com

First Printing 2007

Printed and bound in the United States of America

Library of Congress Control Number: 2007927742
ISBN 978-0-9795985-0-0

This book is dedicated to my father, J. Richard O'Neil Jr.,

a source of wisdom who always encouraged me

to utilize my God given abilities,

and to Robert Gould,

whose imagination and challenges

made me a woodcarver.

Balt Van Tassel was an easy indulgent soul; he loved his daughter better even than his pipe, and, like a reasonable man and an excellent father, let her have her way in everything. His notable little wife, too, had enough to do to attend to her housekeeping and manage her poultry; for, as she sagely observed, ducks and geese are foolish things, and must be looked after, but girls can take care of themselves. Thus, while the busy dame bustled about the house, or plied her spinning-wheel at one end of the piazza, honest Balt would sit smoking his evening pipe at the other, *watching the achievements of a little wooden warrior, who, armed with a sword in each hand, was most valiantly fighting the wind on the pinnacle of the barn.* In the mean time, Ichabod would carry on his suit with the daughter by the side of the spring under the great elm, or sauntering along in the twilight, that hour so favorable to the lover's eloquence.

From *The Legend of Sleepy Hollow* by Washington Irving.   Italics added.

Preface

I had been woodcarving for over twenty years when I attended a New England Woodcarvers meeting that featured a presentation by George MacKinnon on making whirligigs. Mac gave a superb talk, enhanced by his captivating whirligigs which were arrayed on the table before him and which waved and flew in the breeze of a small fan. Afterward, Mac gave me patterns and advice, and I figured I could make whirligigs almost as good as his. The man and the hour had met.

Which is not to say that I quit my job in mechanical engineering and started selling whirligigs for a living. As any aspiring artist or craftsman knows, when you add up the compensation received, and divide by the hours required to make a pleasing piece, you will usually fall short of the federal minimum wage. The first whirligig I made, and every one thereafter, however, behaved exactly as planned and brought squeals and guffaws of delight from their owners and viewers. The demand for whirligigs quickly exceeded the time available to make them. My woodcarving hobby had been considerably enhanced by this new whirligig dimension.

This book is designed first of all for woodcarvers who want to broaden their portfolio and have some real fun at the same time. Those who have never attempted woodcarving, but have experience in making whirligigs will find new ideas and plans, as well as woodcarving techniques to make their creations even more interesting. Moreover, those who have done neither will find all the basic information necessary to get started in both of these rewarding hobbies.

In this book, I have attempted to list all the tools, materials, calculations, plans, sources and techniques for making whirligigs that will work the first time, so that you will not have to "reinvent the whirligig." You may instead concentrate on being artistic and creative. For in crafting whirligigs, like in the old movie about a cross country automobile race, "the rules are: there are no rules." Unlike in the movie, though, we will not throw away the rear view mirror, but will learn from the masters of the past as we dream up new designs that future generations will admire.

Contents

1

Whirligig Design

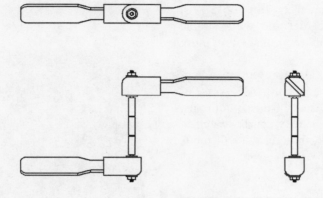

FIGURE 1.1

What is a Whirligig?

What comes to mind when you think of a whirligig? Maybe you draw a blank. My first memories of a whirligig, even before I knew what the word meant, were of a mallard drake mounted on a clothesline pole, with its wings whirling in the breeze.

Perhaps you think of a weathervane with a propeller, mounted on a barn, showing the direction of the wind. Indeed, prior to mid 1930's, it is believed all whirligigs were called "weathervanes". While the word "whirligig" dates to the Middle Ages, it was previously used to describe children's toys, merry-go-rounds or carousels.

Another image of a whirligig might be a little ship by a lighthouse, rocking on a wave as a driving propeller spins in the breeze *(Figure 1.2)*.

The first reference to a whirligig in American literature occurs in *The Legend of Sleepy Hollow* by Washington Irving, initially published in 1819. A man sits on his porch and watches a "little wooden warrior" battle the wind with "a sword in each hand." While not labeled a whirligig, we can easily imagine this device to be a George Washington, a mustachioed Hessian soldier, or some other character of early American folk art design.

Most whirligigs fall into one of these four basic styles: winged, weathervane, mechanical, or arm-waving whirligigs. They all share common characteristics, which include deriving their motion from the wind, indicating the direction of the wind, and providing hours of amusement to their viewers.

Winged Whirligigs

Probably the most prevalent style of whirligigs is the winged whirligig. The most common of these are birds with a two-blade propeller shaped somewhat like a wing on each side. The propeller shafts are screws in each side of the bird and the propellers rotate in opposite directions, which gives the pleasing appearance of wings flapping. The bird is usually a silhouette cut out of a board with a scroll saw, brightly painted and mounted on a nail for a pivot. While the dual propeller designs for these winged whirligigs are not described in this book, the eagle and dragon patterns in Chapters 4 and 5 can be utilized for this style.

Another type of wing design which is suitable for a bird whirligig has one half of the propeller, shaped like a wing on one side, and the other half on the other side, connected by a shaft through the bird. While technically a wing, for the purpose of our discussion, this split-wing design will be considered under the arm-waving category.

Weathervane Whirligigs

As the name suggests, weathervane whirligigs are shaped to point into the wind so that the wind's direction is obvious to the viewer, much like a conventional weathervane. The rotating component is usually a propeller located on the nose. An airplane makes a realistic design, while some creatures with propellers on their noses are more fanciful.

Weathervane whirligigs also present excellent showcases for woodcarving talent. All sorts of subject matter may be used, from mammals, reptiles, birds, fish and bugs to wizards, witches, cars and planes. In this book, though, we will focus on arm waving whirligigs.

FIGURE 1.2

Mechanical Whirligigs

Mechanical whirligigs can be quite intricate. Some rely on a multi-vane propeller which rotates a complex shaft which in turn imparts motion to various characters and objects whose antics entertain us. The subject matter includes men sharpening axes, sailboats bobbing (*Figure 1.2*), women washing and spinning, men driving manual railroad cars, or just about any other action scene

the human mind is capable of inventing. While there are plenty of opportunities for woodcarvers to apply their talents here, and while many of the existing designs would benefit from a woodcarver's expertise, most of the craftsman's effort is funneled into constructing and positioning the various mechanical components to make these whirligigs work.

FIGURE 1.3

Arm-Waving Whirligigs

All the designs in this book can be lumped into one basic category called arm-waving, or split-wing, whirligigs. Whether arms or wings, the propeller is constructed in two pieces located 180 degrees apart and connected by a shaft through the body. The wings or arms are carved at an angle which is the opposite on each side when the wings are assembled.

With the Pegasus shown above (*Figure 1.3*), one can imagine the wings rotating forward when the wind blows towards its right side (into the page). The wind will deflect to the right off the near wing and to the left off the far wing, forcing them to rotate clockwise. If the wind comes from the opposite side, the wings will rotate backwards. If this is hard to visualize now, it will become crystal clear when wing design is discussed in more detail.

Arm-waving whirligigs are mounted on a vertical pin which is located at the correct pivot point, so that the arms always face into the wind.

The pivot is not located directly in line with the shaft for the arms (or wings), but slightly behind it, usually about ¼ inch. The plans for whirligigs in this book show the optimum locations for the shafts and pivots, which will result in the best whirling and gigging. For new designs, however, some experimentation with shaft and pivot location may be necessary to obtain optimum performance.

There are two general styles of arm-waving whirligigs, based on their shape. Some are carved in high relief and some are carved in-the-round. Birds and animals are commonly shaped in silhouette and finished by relief carving (*Figure 1.3*). Humans are usually standing and are fully shaped, which is meant by "carved in-the-round" (*Figure 1.4*).

FIGURE 1.4

Arm-waving figures, usually humans, may also be mounted on a base with some type of tail design so that the arms always face into the wind and rotate in the desired direction. A soldier, for example, may stand on one end of a piece of wood with a mile marker on the other end acting like an airplane's tail, so his arms always rotate forward (*Figure 1.4*). For these designs with a base, the pivot point location is not as important as for designs without this tail. The swords or other devices on the arms, however, must not extend below the feet, to avoid hitting the base plate.

Why Design Whirligigs?

Whirligigs make great gifts. Almost everyone has a back yard, a porch, deck or a fence which receives a little breeze and would benefit from a whirligig. The "person who has everything" doesn't have one of your hand-made works of art. Instead of hunting all over for a $50 gift for your cousin's wedding, make him a whirligig which will not be duplicated or returned, and will provide years of enjoyment.

Whirligigs provide unlimited opportunities to be creative. Your kids, nieces, nephews or grandkids may have a favorite toy or cartoon character that would make an excellent subject for a whirligig. You might like to see King Kong lunging at biplanes. Your backyard could be just the place for a soaring pterodactyl, a sailor signaling a passing ship, the tin man from Oz swinging his ax, a fireman swinging his ax, a policeman or crossing guard with white gloves directing traffic, or an angel catching the breeze.

The fisherman works best in a nor'easter.

FIGURE 1.5

Basic Design Considerations

Whatever style of whirligig is being considered, there are some traditional guidelines that should be followed, especially in the design. They should always be placed outdoors where they will be subjected to the best breeze, their only source of energy. The twirling motion imparted by the wind provides their amusing animation. They should be brightly colored with glossy paint or varnish. They should be visible from the best vantage points, to provide maximum enjoyment.

Inspiration can be derived from the great pieces of Americana located in museums and private collections. While our forebears didn't possess all the materials, tools or know-how that are available to us now, their creations are delightful and worthy of emulation. A few can be seen in the Shelburne Museum (Shelburne, Vermont), Old Sturbridge Village (Massachusetts), and the Henry Ford Museum (Dearborn, Michigan).

Design for Location

Some whirligig designs are more efficient and spin more freely than others. Some locations have more constant breezes and higher average wind speed than others. The wing design and whirligig style can be tailored to fit the planned mounting location.

A back yard in the city surrounded by fences and tall building may receive only slight breezes, in which case the whirligig's arms should be made longer, wider, and thinner in order to increase efficiency. Conversely, a location on a hillside or by the seashore will be subjected to constant blowing, and a less efficient or more unusual wing design may be appropriate.

The surroundings may also influence the whirligig's style. An Indian paddling a birch bark canoe might look lost in a prairie but completely at home in the countryside. A fisherman with yellow oilskins would look great in a harbor setting. A Confederate general might not be appropriate in the inner city.

Materials for Whirligigs

All sorts of materials have been used in whirligig construction. One of the main considerations in material selection must be its durability out of doors (*Figure 1.6*). Different types of wood are probably the most common, but various metals have been utilized with impressive results.

In this book, metals are specified only for the shafts and fasteners, and pine wood is used for the bodies. Other woods noted for their durability may be used, such as redwood, chestnut, teak, and cedar, but for a number of reasons, pine is preferable. Pine is inexpensive and readily available. It is easy to carve, paint and stain, has a beautiful and workable grain, and will last indefinitely when properly finished. It is also fragrant when being carved.

Resist the urge to use Douglas Fir. Fir is cheap, plentiful and rugged, but it is not recommended for wood carving. It has an irregular grain that splits easily and is difficult to carve. Fir may even be mistaken for pine. Basswood and other good carving woods, on the other hand, are not very durable or waterproof. Stick with pine.

There are several types of pine commercially available, each with different characteristics. Some are better for carving; some are more durable. Pine may be called white, yellow, ponderosa, sugar or lodgepole, and each of these types may include several of the 55 species native to North America. Over time a preference for one type may emerge, but the beginner will get great results with virtually any type of pine, properly finished.

The corrosion-proof metals specified in this book are traditional: brass, copper and anodized or galvanized steel. Because of their availability, copper tubing, steel studs, and stainless steel balls are used for the pivot points. Brass is used for shafts, nuts, and washers because of its availability, easy workability, and fine color. Other metals may be substituted without detracting from the functionality of the whirligig, such as stainless steel, bronze, aluminum, and properly finished steel and iron.

One advantage our generation has over the past whirligig masters is plastics. While a traditionalist may ignore plastics altogether, the material is very useful for bushings. The designs in this book all include white nylon bushings and washers which should unobtrusively keep the arms and wings spinning freely for years.

Whatever your preference in materials, each design shown in this book lists all the recommended parts. Feel free to substitute and experiment.

FIGURE 1.6

Propellers – Arm and Wing Design

There are two major challenges in making whirligigs – finding a design that works properly, and making sure it keeps on working while constantly exposed to all sorts of weather conditions. While the fabrication techniques and twenty-first century materials described in this book will insure rugged construction and longevity, one of the most daunting tasks of whirligig design for expert and neophyte alike, can be laying out the arms or wings.

If the rule of thumb for carpentry is "measure twice and cut once," for whirligig arms it should be "measure, think, and analyze about five times before removing material." Yet the basic concept is simple – you just have to force yourself to stop and think about it.

FIGURE 1.7

The fisherman (*Figure 1.5*) has relatively simple arms with oars on the ends. Both arms are identical, (*Figure 1.7*) with the outside of the shoulder rounded and the inside flat. The oars are cut at an angle in the block of wood, from one edge to the opposite edge. When they are assembled on a shaft 180 degrees apart, with the insides of the shoulders facing each other, the oars become blades at opposite angles and they make an effective propeller *(Figure 1.8)*. If the oars are made with their angles reversed, the arms will spin in the opposite direction from oars cut at the original angle.

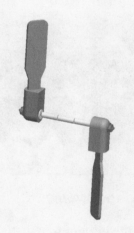

FIGURE 1.8

While not all whirligigs have left and right arms or wings which are identical or symmetrical, they must all have the same relationship between the angle of the blade and the inside of the shoulder. The boxer in Chapter 8, for example, has arms which are bent forward slightly at the elbows. Therefore, the biceps are rounded at the front of the shoulder on one side, and at the back of the shoulder on the other (*Figure 8.1*). The plans in this book will show the design clearly, but during construction some thought will be required. It always helps to keep a pencil handy, and to sketch on the arm where material is to be removed or retained. The arms should be marked "left" and "right" and the inside identified at all times. When part of the marking has been carved off, it should be redrawn again before too long.

The Pivot Point

For whirligig arms or wings to spin, the shaft must be in line with the wind direction. The whirligig must be designed so that the body rotates broadside to the wind as the wind direction changes. The whirligig is mounted, and rotates, on a pivot pin - usually a large nail or spike with its head cut off. The body will have a hole for the pivot pin, sometimes lined with a copper tube, in the middle between the right and left sides. The correct front-to-back location for this hole is called the pivot point.

For the designs in this book, a stainless steel ball is inserted into this hole above the copper tube to insure the whirligig rotates freely on the pivot point.

Locating the pivot is not an exact science, and for new designs an educated guess usually works right the first time. The pivot point should be about ¼ inch behind the hub of the shaft. It might seem intuitive to mount the pivot in the center of the body, or at the center of gravity of the body, or in line with the hub, but these locations generally don't allow the whirligig to orient itself into the wind so that the arms rotate freely.

Wing Bases

Some whirligig designs have arms or wings which would normally collide with the mounting base or part of the whirligig's body, especially those carved in high relief. To prevent this, a small block of wood, called a wing base, is glued or screwed to the body on each side, acting as a stand-off. These can be seen on Pegasus (*Figure 1.3*) and the fisherman (*Figure 1.5*), where the wing bases appear to be his shoulders. Standing figures carved in-the-round (*Figure 1.4*) don't need wing or arm bases attached, but may require broad shoulders to avoid arm scraping.

Mounting Bases

Another important consideration in whirligig design is how to mount it. How it is mounted might also depend on where it is mounted. The main design considerations for bases are: they should be sturdy, durable, hold the pivot pin, and allow clearance for the arms or wings to spin.

FIGURE 1.9

A popular location for a whirligig is on the railing of a porch or deck. A simple assembly comprising two pieces of pressure-treated lumber screwed into the railing with two deck screws, with a pivot pin pressed in the top *(Figure 1.9)* makes an effective mounting base. The base finish can be left natural, varnished, or painted to match the porch.

A whirligig mounted on a picket fence might have a base made from the top of another picket. This piece can be screwed into one of the pickets on the fence with deck screws, with a pivot pin pressed in between.

Sketch an Original Design

Conventional artistic ability and formal training are not required for creating a good piece of folk art. To make an original whirligig, a full size pattern is essential. Sketch the profile shape of your subject. In some cases, a picture – like a profile view from a bird guide - can be photocopied and enlarged on the copier to the right size, and then traced. Mark the locations for the arms or wings, with the point for the shaft through the shoulders. Wings are usually located in a realistic manner, although shaft holes for human arms may be

slightly forward and lower in the shoulder for strength and pivot point optimization.

For full-bodied designs, the front view may be sketched beside the side profile, with the features lining up horizontally. This will aid in designing the arms to clear the body and base. This view can also be used as a pattern for cutting the body out of the block of wood. If a wing base is required, sketch it in also.

Sketch the outline of the arms or wings. Human arms, without swords attached, may be longer or wider than normal proportions. Wings are usually sized realistically. Make sure the arms/wings will be exposed to adequate air flow on both sides. An end view of the wing may be helpful, showing the angle of the propeller blade.

On the side view of the body, locate the proposed location for the pivot point, about ¼ inch behind the wing shaft. Use the patterns in this book for reference.

Time to Think About Construction

With all this in mind, it's time to consider construction techniques. Don't forget that these design guidelines, however, are only that: guidelines. Any new improvements to the whirligig body of knowledge, which will bring a little pleasure to those who appreciate this fine art, will be greatly welcome.

FIGURE 1.10

There is one whirligig rule that should never be broken: *mount your whirligig outdoors!* If, to the contrary, nothing moves on your creation; if you've spent weeks and months carving it; if it's made of a non-durable material like basswood; if it's painted a dull, realistic color *(Figure 1.10)* – you will be forgiven for mounting it in your den. But if it's a whirligig, then set it free outside.

6

2

Whirligig Construction

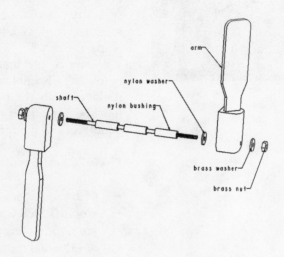

FIGURE 2.1

Turning Ideas into Reality

So now we have a design. It may be a swimmer, or a shark chasing a swimmer, or Sam Adams hoisting a beer. It may be a Civil War general or our favorite bird of prey. It could be a huge, fiendish hound chasing poor Sir Henry Baskerville. We have sketched our pattern, and we have worked out a good location for the arm shaft and the pivot point. We are fairly certain that our design will point into the wind and respond to most slight breezes. Now we have to transform our brainstorm into a whirligig which will look as good and perform as well next year in our back yard as it does this week on our basement workbench. It is time to consider construction techniques.

It's not easy to say where design actually ends and construction begins. Many of the challenges to be faced in whirligig construction should have been thought through in the design phase. Since all of the whirligigs presented in this book have already been designed, the subjects touched upon in this chapter will be considered construction topics. If you are designing an original whirligig, however, you might want to plan for some of the contingencies mentioned here in your design phase.

Construction Tools

Before starting any project, it's always a good idea to round up some of the tools and supplies you will need to have on hand. The items on the list below and their uses will be described in this and the next chapter. Where possible, alternatives are suggested.

Many of these tools are not essential for making quality whirligigs, but they can make the process quicker and easier. I can think of many whirligigs and woodcarvings that I've made without a band saw and more than a few stands and mounts I've made without using a table saw or drill press (*Figure 2.2*); they may have taken a few minutes longer to make, but they all came out fine. Therefore, while I'm not recommending you run out and buy a cordless drill, I do think there are certain gadgets that will remove much tedium and help you to be productive and creative. The following components are useful:

FIGURE 2.2

Useful Tools and Supplies

- Artist paint brushes
- Band saw, scroll saw
- Chisels
- Clamps
- Coping saw
- Cutting fluid (like Tap Majic from the Steco Corporation)
- Die for #6-32 (UNC-2A) thread & handle
- Dremel motor tool & bits
- Drill bits
- Drill press
- Electric drill, 3/8 inch, variable speed, reversible
- Files
- Hacksaw
- Hammer
- Jig saw or saber saw
- Rasps
- Rifflers
- Sandpaper, garnet or aluminum oxide, 60 coarse, 100 medium, 150 fine, 220 very fine
- Screwdrivers
- Sharpening stones
- Table fan
- Table saw
- Vice
- Vice grips type pliers
- Wood carving gouges
- Wood carving knife
- Wrenches, including 5/16" box and open end

Sources of Supplies

Most of the tools and materials required for whirligig construction can be found at the local hardware store, lumber yard, building supply center, department or craft store. Depending where you live, some items may only be available through mail order. Woodcarving tools like gouges and small rifflers are available from companies that specialize in these products, and a number of them are listed in the Appendices. Small tools, bushings and fasteners can be obtained from Small Parts Inc., and sources for specialty tools can be obtained from the manufacturers. These addresses are also listed in the Appendices.

Some of the materials in the list of components below are also not mandatory, and can be omitted or replaced with alternate parts. Outstanding whirligigs have been made in the last two centuries without the benefit of our modern technology.

Useful Components

- #6 brass flat washers
- #6 brass lock washers
- #6-32 brass thread inserts (or use nuts)
- #6-32 brass nuts
- 1/8 inch diameter brass rod
- brass wood screws (various sizes as required)
- copper tube 3/8" outside diameter (OD)
- deck screws, 8 x 2 ½" long, 7 x 1 5/8" long
- epoxy, 2 part and epoxy putty
- exterior paints, high gloss
- exterior primer, white acrylic latex
- Loctite Thread Locker (Loctite Corp, Rocky Hill, CT)
- nails or spikes, ¼" DIA, 4 to 6" long
- nylon bushings (.140" ID x .250" OD x .75" long; also ½ & 1" long)
- nylon flat washers & wide flat washers, #6
- pine wood 1 inch thick (.75" actual) & 2 inch thick (1.50" actual)
- pressure treated wood for stands
- stainless steel balls, 5/16 DIA
- wood glue, exterior
- wood seal, clear preservative

Durability

Whirligigs are meant to be left outside all year round. My mentor, Mac MacKinnon, left his whirligigs out in hurricanes. Those who don't have the ability to repair hurricane damage might consider bringing them inside if the eye of the storm is within a hundred miles or so. If there are tornado warnings, your whirligig's safety should be the last thing on your mind. In all other weather conditions, though, your designs should be constructed to endure outdoors.

The materials listed here will provide sufficient robustness for all weather conditions. One extremely windy day I came home to find my fisherman whirligig (*Figure 1.5*) gone and its base badly damaged. It had been mounted on the railing of my deck, which is about twelve feet above ground level. Upon investigation, it was determined that a large branch broke off the maple tree above the deck and knocked the whirligig to the ground. A bent shaft was the only damage, and I decided to replace the shaft to insure continued optimum performance.

If you intend to substitute any materials from those suggested here, consider their strength and durability first.

Construction Techniques

Using a drill press is the best way to insure that holes will be drilled at the desired locations and angles. A table saw will provide the smooth, straight cuts for clean surfaces. If these tools are unavailable, hand held drills and saws will work fine with a little extra effort and attention to detail.

The proper safety procedures for operating power woodworking equipment should be followed. A pusher should always be used to guide the work piece through a table saw. Wear safety goggles and a dust mask when using power tools.

Care should be taken to insure drilled holes are the correct size, located properly and at the right angle. The fits of the shaft and bushings, the pivot pin and its sleeve do not have to be perfect for satisfactory performance. Woodworking is a relatively painless and forgiving endeavor. Many mistakes can be easily covered up or corrected, and perfection is not necessary for a first class whirligig.

Wood Sizes for Whirligigs

Lumber is sold in nominal sizes with either rough or finished surfaces. Rough boards can be used for making whirligigs and woodcarvings, but finished lumber is preferable. With a rough or saw cut finish, the outside layer will have to be cleaned away to obtain a smooth workable surface. Finished, or dressed, lumber has been planed smooth and is ready to use as-is, or to be laminated into thicker pieces.

The actual size of finished lumber will always be smaller than the nominal size. Therefore, a one inch board will actually be three-quarters of an inch thick.

A 2 x 4 will actually be 1 ½ X 3 ½ inches. As a general rule to determine the actual size of dressed lumber, subtract ¼ inch from the nominal size (thickness and width) for lumber under two inches; ½ inch for sizes two to seven inches, and ¾ inches for larger sizes.

The quantity of lumber sold is measured in board-feet. One board foot is the equivalent to a one inch thick by twelve inches wide by twelve inches long, nominal size, piece of board. A foot long piece of 2 x 6 board, for example, will equal one board foot. A board foot of one by four lumber will be three feet long. For your homework, determine the number of board feet in a three inch by fourteen inch by ten foot long piece of wood (the answer is at the bottom of page 35).

Gluing and Laminating

The bodies for the high relief designs in this book – the eagle and dragon – and all the arms and wings can be made from one-inch nominal pine. The human figures carved in-the-round – the knight, boxer and soldier – require two inch thick or larger pine wood, which is not as easy to find as one inch lumber. Two or more pieces of thinner wood may be glued together to make a larger piece as an acceptable alternative.

Three pieces of one-inch finished stock, which is actually ¾ inch thick, when glued together will give a 2 ¼ inch block of wood. The three pieces can be cut from the same board, and assembled with the grain running in the same direction. Make sure there are no knots or surface imperfections. Apply good exterior wood glue to the joints and clamp tightly with wood clamps, or apply a heavy weight evenly on the pieces. When the glue is dry, the laminated block may be cut, carved and painted. The seams will be invisible, and no one will be the wiser.

Some designs require wing blocks to prevent the wings from hitting the side of the body or the mounting base. These can be assembled by gluing as well as with screws. The wood surfaces should be flat and clean. Apply good exterior wood glue and clamp tightly.

Epoxy can also be useful. If, for example, the hole for a pivot tube is drilled at the wrong angle, it can be redrilled and the tube can be assembled in the hole with two-part epoxy putty. This will harden solid and hold the tube at the correct angle, and it may then be carved or drilled and painted.

Making Shafts

1/8 inch brass rod is the ideal shaft material for whirligigs of the size shown in this book. It is cut to the proper length with a hack saw, and the edges should be cleaned up – deburred – with a file. Threads are added to one or both ends with a #6-32 die and handle (*Figure 2.3*). Brass is relatively soft, so cutting the threads is easy with a drop of cutting fluid added to the shaft.

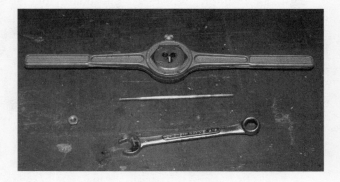

FIGURE 2.3

The main challenge is holding the shaft so it doesn't rotate instead of the die. The shaft may end up scored from a firm hold by a vice/vice grips unless a piece of rubber is used as a liner. Any vice marks can be sanded smooth afterwards.

When the shaft is gripped firmly, cut thread on the end about ¾ inches long by turning the die slowly, backing off occasionally and rethreading. Be careful not to bend or twist the shaft as you apply pressure to make the threads.

Alternate Shaft Construction

The most problematical component of arm-waving whirligigs is the shaft for the arms or wings. By definition, whirligigs should have moving parts, and there is nothing more frustrating than building a whirligig that doesn't spin. Sometimes, sooner or later, either the shaft binds up or the arms lose their alignment and come loose. There is no foolproof method for making shafts that don't require some measure of maintenance.

All designs are compromises, and whirligig shafts are no exception. If you want a shaft that doesn't bind up, or that can be removed for whirligig repair and maintenance, then eventually the arms or wings will loosen and performance will degrade. If the shaft binds, warps or swells, or the shaft hole shrinks, or the arms warp and hit the body, you shouldn't have to

drill out the shaft to fix things. If, however, you assemble the arms to stay aligned permanently, then drastic measures will be required to fix even a minor interference problem.

The shafts described in this book are designed and constructed for easy disassembly. Consequently, the arms/wings may lose alignment, and periodic adjustment may be necessary. Innovative shaft designs can be utilized to eliminate or minimize this problem, but these concepts are beyond the scope of this book.

One way to minimize the loosening of the wings or arms is to thread only one end of the shaft, and to glue the other end permanently into one arm. You can even file a flat on this end, and press it into a smaller hole in the arm along with some glue or epoxy to insure it never becomes loose. This step shouldn't be taken until all the final carving and adjustment has been made to the arm. This will also aid in tightening the other arm, as sometimes both arms tend to turn together when tightening one end with both ends threaded.

Numerous other shaft designs have been used in making whirligigs, and you are welcome to try out other configurations. Instead of using nylon bushings as bearings for the shaft, a quarter inch diameter brass tube cut slightly longer than the body width may be pressed into a ¼ inch hole through the shoulders. Use a 3/16 inch diameter brass rod for this shaft. A brass bushing will cause more friction and wear than a nylon bushing.

For some designs, the shaft end isn't threaded, but is pressed into holes in the arms and glued. Alternately, wooden dowels may be used for shafts. These will make a good joint in the arm, which will never loosen if glued correctly, but swelling, warping and wear will shorten the whirligig's lifetime.

Painting

Most whirligigs parts require a coating all over with a good outdoor primer, probably white, and two coats of a decent gloss outdoor paint, water or oil based. Since the only features not painted will be the holes, a coat hanger or some other wire can be inserted in the holes and used to hold or hang the piece during painting and drying.

For some unknown reason, some colors cover better than others, so care should be taken to stay within the lines when painting adjacent features. Since most whirligigs will only be viewed at a distance, less intricate detail will be required in the final paint job.

3

Woodcarving for Whirligig Makers

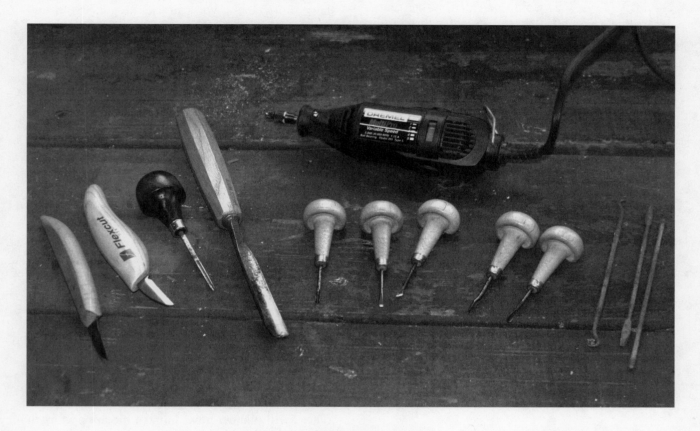

FIGURE 3.1

Woodcarving Basics

Experienced woodcarvers can skip this chapter. I'm sure many could teach me a thing or two. I'm also sure many would agree when I say that if *I* can do woodcarving, then anyone can. I could never have done it when I was ten years old and immature, though some really great carvings are done by youngsters. With age, though, comes patience, probably the main attribute of a good carver.

To me, there is no such thing as a bad woodcarving – some are superior to others, but all are pleasing to view, and the texture, grain and versatility of wood almost guarantee a satisfactory result.

By now, there should be no expert woodcarvers reading this chapter, which is fortunate for me. If the Woodcarvers Guild found out I was giving away all their secrets and showing how simple woodcarving really can be, they would send over a punk named Gepetto to break my thumbs.

The following are a few simple concepts, rules and tricks most, if not all, woodcarvers use to remove the excess wood which is covering the creation which already exists in their block of wood. Keep these in mind, keep practicing and observing, and you will soon be carving like an expert.

In-the-Round and Relief Carving

Most woodcarvings can be described as either in-the-round or relief. In-the-round carvings generally depict a full, three dimensional representation of the subject. A full size, realistic sculpture of a religious figure in a church, for example, is considered in-the-round. A decoy carving (*Figure 3. 2*) would be called in-the-round, as are the soldier, boxer and knight whirligigs in this book.

FIGURE 3.2

Relief carvings are foreshortened depictions of a subject that, while not fully three-dimensional, give the impression of realistic depth. Some carvings which are not much more than raised sketches of a subject are considered low relief. High relief carvings have much more depth of field, and some come close to being in-the-round (*Figure 3.3*). The eagle and dragon whirligigs in this book are high relief.

FIGURE 3.3

Use Patterns

Before beginning any carving, it is best to have pictures and sketches of your subject from different angles, and if possible models, specimens and study bills of birds. There will usually be one preferred profile view to use for a pattern. When the pattern is traced on a block of wood and cut out with a band saw, you are already half way towards your desired shape. For starters, you can use the patterns in this book, and as you gain experience, you can make your own patterns.

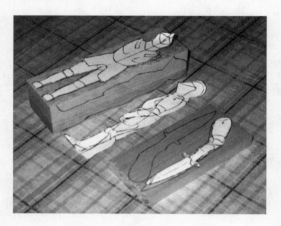

FIGURE 3.4

Sometimes two patterns can be used for a carving, such as the standing human figures for whirligigs. Trace the side profile on the side of a block of wood and the front profile on the front surface (*Figure 3.4*). Cut the side profile with a band saw and reattach the pieces with small nails or a few dabs of super glue. Lay the block on its back and cut the front profile. The idea is to remove as much wood and to come as close to the final shape as possible before you start carving.

Draw a Centerline

Once the profile shape has been cut from a block of wood using a pattern, sketch a line with pencil all around the center of the work piece. This line will go through the center of the nose, mouth, torso, back and so forth to . help keep the carving symmetrical. This line will help you to maintain the eyes centered in the head and to ensure both sides of the carving are rounded evenly.

Since the centerline is on the profile shape, it will usually not be carved away until the end when the finishing cuts are being made. If a portion of the line has to be carved off, sketch it back on as soon as possible.

Sketch Details on the Work Piece

Pencil marks are easily erased and will not permanently stain the wood like ink will. Use a pencil and sketch all the features on the work piece which will aid in visualizing the final carving. Locate and sketch eyes, mouth, teeth, legs, etc. on the work piece to help locate your cuts. From time to time, as the marks are cut away, sketch them back as you get closer to the final shape. This will help you make the parts the right shape in the right location, and to maintain symmetry.

Study the Grain

The grain generally runs parallel to the length of a board of wood. Carvings are best made with the grain running parallel to the length of the carving, since this is the easiest way to carve, and features are the strongest "with" the grain. On a bird the grain should run from the bill to the tail. On a human figure, the grain will run from head to foot. A nose for example will be much sturdier with the grain running from top to bottom than across it.

The bill of the eagle is more delicate. It is easier to carve the whole eagle with the grain running from head to tail, and the tail is stronger this way. This leaves the tip of the bill, however, which is short and pointed downward, running across the grain. Likewise the feet of human figures usually are at right angles to the grain, making the toes weaker. On indoor woodcarvings these delicate, cross grain features should be carved carefully and slowly, and maybe given a good soaking of super glue. For outdoor whirligigs, they should be carved a little thicker and wider for durability.

Grain influences the way cuts are made to shape features. Grain does not flow in even, straight lines, but changes direction and shifts along the length of the wood. Carving is easier along and down "with" the grain and more difficult or nearly impossible up into end grain. Carving is sometimes easy in one direction along the beginning of a contour until the direction changes into the grain, and then the cuts will have to be made from the other direction. This will become apparent when, instead of making clean, smooth chips, you are digging in and splitting the wood. Sometimes one side of a head can be carved like butter while the other side requires some major contortions and different tools due to the grain direction. Proceed slowly with initial cuts until the lay of the grain is determined.

Cut Away From Yourself

When woodcarvers get together, we proudly show off our scars. I can only find one good one now, but cuts are a constant occupational hazard which should be minimized. Using sharp tools, somewhat surprisingly, makes carving safer. Dull tools can snag or slip, with dangerous results, while sharp tools are easier to control. The most important rule to follow is to hold your tool in the right position, and cut in the right direction so that there are no body parts in the path of the blade. Then if the wood breaks, or the blade slips, the force of the stroke will carry the blade away from your body.

It is still possible when cutting away from yourself to have the blade slip and the carving spin around so that the blade heads for flesh. It is important therefore to start out slowly and use controlled strokes, bearing in mind what will happen with a slip. The work piece should always be held firmly or anchored securely. Some carvings can be held in vices or screwed into various types of "power arms" which can be repositioned and locked easily. Chisel and gouge cuts can be made with the work piece on a bench positioned up against a hard stop, like a block of wood.

Sometimes it is necessary to cut toward yourself to achieve the correct shape. Use short controlled strokes with constant attention to the minimum amount of force necessary to make the cut and to insure the blade will not travel any further if there is a slip.

Rough Out, Then Finish

All woodcarvings go through several stages. Once the blank has been cut out of the board or block of wood, the next stage is a general rounding or roughing out of the shape. The major features and the centerline are sketched on the work piece and larger, coarser tools are used to quickly remove material to arrive at the rough shape. There can be several rough stages as the carving is gradually taken down closer to the final shape.

It is important not to add too much detail to one feature while ignoring the rest. It is better to go around the carving, or back and forth, roughing out the features at the same rate, keeping them at all the same relative level of completion and maintaining symmetry.

A common beginner's mistake is to stop roughing out the carving too soon. These carvings have a rectangular, boxy appearance with rounded corners. Experienced carvers are not afraid to take the carving down to a realistic shape. In all of my carvings, I can't ever remember taking off too much material, but I can recall carvings which would have benefited from a few more cuts. Don't be afraid to make that one last cut.

Once you are satisfied the carving is fairly close to the final shape, the detail carving can commence. Again it is advisable to add detail evenly around the carving, not concentrating too much in one area at a time, and check symmetry. In determining the level of detail, you should take into consideration how the carving will be mounted. Whirligigs generally will be mounted outside and viewed at a distance, which will allow a lower level of detail, and greater ruggedness, to be acceptable.

Carvings can be sanded smooth or left with varying amounts of tool marks. If sanded, start with the coarser grades of paper (lower grade number) making sure the coarse paper doesn't leave scrape marks which can't be easily smoothed out by the less coarse paper. Work down to the finest grade (highest grade number) for the finished surface.

If the carving is left unsanded, the tool marks should be smooth and spaced evenly. It is better not to partially sand the tool marks as this only makes the carving look lumpy. Except for certain areas, like faces and wing surfaces, and the knight's armor, I prefer not to sand my whirligigs. The carving marks are not visible at a short distance, and give a nice folk art appearance up close. This also saves a lot of time.

Stop and Look

Whether your carving is in the rough or finish stage, you should periodically stop, step back, and review what you've accomplished. Look at the carving from many different angles with varying light sources. Observe your work in natural, incandescent and fluorescent light. Check symmetry and shape, and compare the work piece with your sketches and references. Analyze proportions – are the arms coming out longer than the legs? Make new pencil markings on the carving to guide your next cuts. Ensure the centerline is visible, and continue with your carving.

Carving with Power Tools

Some woodcarvers use power tools exclusively when they carve, while some traditionalists only use hand tools. Others, like me, use a combination of tools depending on the situation, and the alignment of the planets. Both methods of carving have

advantages although there is virtually nothing one method can do that the other can't.

The direction of the grain is much less of a concern for power tool carvers, since the bits can grind down through the wood in any direction. The smaller bits can reach places that are difficult for gouges or knives. For these reasons, I like to put down the hand tools and use a power carver with a small ball bit to open up the dragon's mouth or to cut through the blank to make space between a soldier's legs.

I prefer power tools for carving hard woods. With ebony, maple, oak, or even walnut, hand tools require more effort, not to mention sharpening time. For most woods, though, I've found that an equivalent cut with either style tool removes an equivalent amount of wood. The difference is that a gouge cut leaves a nice, clean chip, while with a power tool cut, half the wood goes up your nose and the other half settles like snow on every object in the room. Attaching the shop vacuum near the work piece helps keep down the dust. Wear a dust mask and goggles while using power tools. How to keep the goggles from fogging up while wearing a dust mask will be the subject of my next book.

The power tool and the work piece have to be held securely since the rotating bit has a tendency to act like a wheel and to "walk" in the direction of rotation, leaving nasty chatter marks along the length of your carving, or obliterating the subject's nose or bill.

Carving with Hand Tools

A good knife or two designed for woodcarving, a set of small or miniature gouges, a V-parter, chisels, a skew chisel, rasps and a set of assorted rifflers should be more than enough to carve good whirligigs (*Figure 3.1*). The exact size and shape of these tools that are right for you will have to be determined by experience. As you develop your own personal preferences, you will find some tools are used very rarely, while others get constant use. For the whirligig carvings in this book, the smaller tools will work better while full size gouges won't see too much action. Sources of wood carving tools are listed in the Appendices.

When first buying gouges and other shaped carving tools, make sure they come sharpened to the finished configuration. Many high quality tools come unfinished and require grinding and initial sharpening by an experienced hand. Beginners should avoid using a grinding wheel to shape and sharpen tools. When done improperly, grinding heats, or anneals, the tool and softens the steel so that it won't hold it's edge as long.

For carving fine detail around eyes, bills, fingers, etc. a set of assorted bent riffler rasps is indispensable *(on the right of Figure 3.1)*. These versatile tools can safely and easily remove wood where knives either can't reach or can't be trusted to make a real fine cut. Sometimes sandpaper can be used to bring fine detail down to the final shape. With these tools, the direction of the grain is not a problem.

Keep Your Hand Tools Sharp

Okay, maybe there is one part of woodcarving which some people consider difficult or boring, but experienced woodcarvers consider essential. All your knives and gouges should be constantly kept sharp. Admittedly, this is a rule that is easier said than done. This chore may be one reason for the popularity of power carving tools, whose bits last quite a while and cannot be sharpened by a layman. If you are using power tools for carving, skip this section.

One way to avoid the effort of sharpening and to acquire a quick set of woodcarving tools is to use replaceable knife and gouge blades with matching handles, such as the Exacto style product line. The inexpensive blades come in all sizes and shapes, and are quite sharp right out of the box. They can still be resharpened, but replacing them is even easier.

How frequently you should sharpen is a matter of opinion, but tools should be sharpened at the very least before each carving session. They should be sharpened when they no longer produce a clean, crisp cut in the wood. The harder the wood being carved, the more often sharpening will be needed. The better quality the steel of the tool, the less sharpening will be required. The hardness of tool steel is usually graded in the Rockwell "C" Scale, the higher the number, the harder the steel. Look for knives and gouges in the Rc 55 to Rc 63 range. With experience you will be better able to tell when the quality of the cuts is becoming unsatisfactory, and it is time to sharpen. This could be as often as every 15 minutes.

Sharpening should be done manually on coarse, medium and fine sharpening stones with honing oil applied, followed by stropping on a leather strop. If the edge is in relatively good shape, start with the medium or fine stone, or merely strop. If it's rounded and nicked, start with the coarse stone.

Make sure a drop or two of oil is applied to the stone surface to help float away the metal chips. Note the angle of the edges of the blade, hold the tool so the same angle will be maintained and draw the edge back and forth across the flat stone keeping the angle constant. With gouges and other tools that don't have a straight edge, slowly and evenly rotate the edge as you draw the tool across the stone. It might help to mark the edge surfaces with a magic marker. After several strokes, observe where the marker ink is removed. Fixtures are available commercially to help maintain the proper sharpening angle.

With knives, repeat sharpening on the other side. After several strokes, examine the edge closely. The correct angle of the point should have been maintained, and there will be some burrs on the edge. Repeat the process with the finer stone. For gouges and vee tools, rounded or angled stones are required for the inside edge.

When you are satisfied with the new edge from stoning, strop the blade to remove the large burrs and make a smooth point. A piece of a leather belt nailed to a small board makes a good strop. If honing compound is available, apply some to the strop. Draw the blade across the strop several times at the correct angle, in one direction with the sharp edge trailing. Do not push the blade forward as you would on a stone as this will obviously damage the strop.

Stropping removes the large burrs and creates a fine knife edge with microscopic burrs or steel molecules which actually do the cutting. Some carvers rarely use stones, but strop frequently with a good honing compound to maintain the correct edge.

Once the tools are sharp, protect the edges from contact with hard or abrasive surfaces. Touching sandpaper, concrete or other tools will quickly damage the microscopic edge and undo your sharpening effort. Store tools in a wooden box or a case with individual canvas or leather pockets.

Sharpening is an art in itself, and there are entire books devoted to the skill. With a little experience, you will find that you can quickly improve your cutting edges, and carving will become much easier.

4

The Bald Eagle Whirligig

FIGURE 4.1

Notes on the Design

I was hesitant to do a bald eagle at first because this bird doesn't meet one of the basic rules of whirligig design: it isn't very colorful. Since these rules are made to be broken, however, and since I admire these beautiful birds, I sketched the plans, went to work and was pleasantly surprised with the results.

This is the most efficient whirligig I've made to date. This bird almost flies off its pivot point in a medium breeze, although it's been known to fly backward. The original size plans, at eight inches long, make a simple and straightforward project, utilizing one inch by four-inch pine stock (¾ x 3- ½" actual size).

Like all the other plans in this book, this design can be scaled up or down with the use of a photocopier. While I wouldn't shrink it, there is no limit to the size this eagle could be (well, maybe six feet would be excessive). If true one inch or 1¼" stock can be found, a 12 to 24 inch long eagle would look great. For a larger whirligig, a 3/16 inch diameter shaft threaded #10-24 or a ¼ inch diameter shaft threaded 1/4-20 might be a good idea. A bigger bird also means more carving time and effort, of course, which would be more than compensated by the praise of neighbors living four blocks away.

The Bald Eagle Pattern

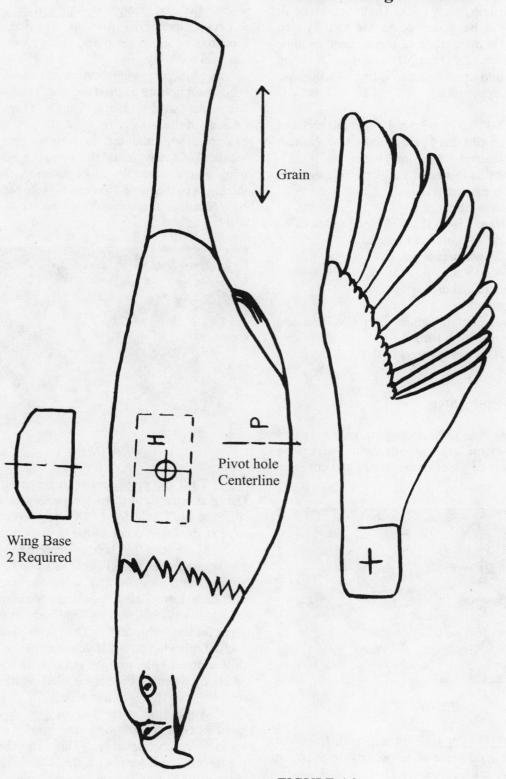

Grain

Pivot hole
Centerline

Wing Base
2 Required

FIGURE 4.2

List of Material

This list includes all the material necessary to make this whirligig by the book. The functions of all these items will be described in the step-by-step instructions. Alternate material can be used in most cases. The shaft, for example, could be a wood dowel, glued into the wings and riding in a bushing made from a copper tube.

1. (1) 1 x 4 x 12" (.75 x 3.5 x 12" actual) piece of seasoned or kiln dried pine wood, or equivalent
2. (1) 1/8" diameter x 4 ½" long brass rod
3. (1) 3/8 Outside Diameter x 1" long copper tube
4. (4) #6-32 brass nuts
5. (2) #6 brass washers
6. (3) .140 I.D x .250 O.D. x .75" long nylon tubes or bushings, or equivalent lengths
7. (2) #6 nylon washers
8. Exterior wood glue
9. Loctite thread locker
10. Exterior primer
11. Dark brown, bright white, bright yellow and black exterior gloss paint
12. (1) 5/16 DIA stainless steel ball
13. Sandpaper

Bald Eagle Step-by-Step

1. <u>Make a pattern.</u> Photocopy or trace the plans *(Figure 4.2)* of the eagle's body, wings and wing bases on a sheet of paper or cardboard and cut them out.

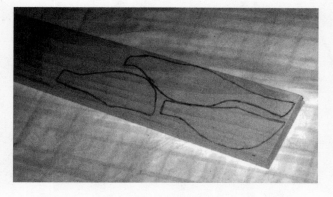

FIGURE 4.3

2. <u>Lay out the parts.</u> With a pencil, trace the shapes onto a good piece of wood, paying attention to the grain direction *(Figure 4.3)*.

3. <u>Cut out the parts.</u> Using a band saw, coping saw, scroll saw, jig saw or saber saw, cut out the body, 2 wings and 2 wing bases.

4. <u>Mark the location of holes on the body.</u> With a pencil, using the plan as a guide, mark the locations of the pivot point, wing bases, and wing shaft on the body.

5. <u>Mark the wings.</u> Mark the location of the wing shaft hole on each of the wings and wing bases. Mark the shape of the wing's propeller blade on each of the wings *(Figure 4.4)*. Note that for this example, both the left and right wings will be identical. Clearly mark the opposite edges of the wing where material will be retained, showing the thickness of the wing – about 1/8 inch. Near the shaft hole location, mark each wing on the inside "left" and "right".

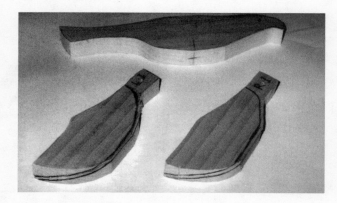

FIGURE 4.4

6. <u>Drill the pivot and shaft holes in the body.</u> Using an electric drill or (preferably) a drill press, drill the 3/8" hole by 1 1/8" deep for the copper tube at the pivot point in the bottom of the eagle's body. Make sure this hole is centered in the wood, and enters at the correct angle as shown on the plan. If necessary, measure and put masking tape on the drill bit to insure the proper depth is maintained.

Drill a ¼" hole through the body at the marked point for the wing shaft. Drill a ¼" hole through each of the wing bases. If you are confident you can drill a clean hole straight through the wing bases and body when they are assembled together, you can omit these ¼" holes at this time.

7. <u>Attach the wing bases to the body.</u> Apply good exterior wood glue to the insides of the wing bases. Attach one on each side of the body where the marking indicates, with the ¼" holes aligned (a nail through all three pieces may help the alignment). Clamp the pieces tightly, making sure

nothing slides around, and allow to dry *(Figure 4.5)*. In lieu of a clamp, weights may be used, or a bolt with flat washers may be inserted and tightened in the hole for the shaft. Instead of the whole gluing procedure, if you prefer, brass or stainless steel screws may be used to attach the wing bases.

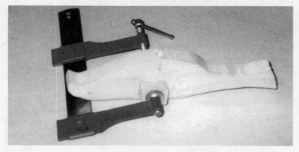

FIGURE 4.5

8. <u>Drill a hole for the shaft in the wing.</u> Drill a 3/32" hole through the wings at the shaft location.

If you want to get fancy, you may install threaded inserts in the wings to help keep them locked in position, although this step is not necessary. If conventional threaded inserts are to be used in the wings, drill the pilot hole in the outside of the shoulder area (do birds have shoulders?). To use a nut for an insert, drill a 9/32" hole about 1/8" deep. Screw a #6-32 threaded shaft (if one is not available, see step 10) through the wing as a guide, so that it extends slightly beyond the outside surface. Screw the nut on the shaft and carefully hammer the nut into the 9/32" hole until it is flush with the surface. Remove the shaft.

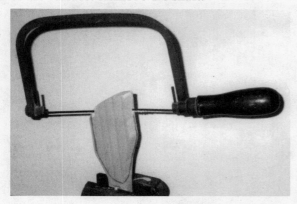

FIGURE 4.6

9. <u>Rough out the wings.</u> Using a band saw, coping saw, jig saw, chisels, knives or gouges, carefully remove the material from both sides of the wings to make a propeller vane about 1/8" thick *(Figure 4.6)*. With a knife, round off the outside of the shoulders. At this point, both wings should be relatively smooth and very close in size, shape and weight. Carving of feather detail should wait until after the wings are tested in step 13.

10. <u>Make the shaft.</u> With a hacksaw, cut a 4-½ inch long piece of 1/8" diameter brass rod. Using a file, round off and deburr the edges. Thread each end about ½ inch long with a #6-32 die *(Figure 2.3)*. One way to do this is clamp the rod in the middle with vice-grip pliers, and set the vice-grips on a vice for further stability. Apply some cutting fluid to the rod and die, and carefully screw the die down the rod, backing off once in a while, being careful not to bend the shaft. Unscrew the die, flip the vice-grips over and repeat for the other side. Remove the vice-grips and lightly sand any indentations they may have made in the shaft.

As an alternative, make the shaft slightly shorter and thread only one end. File a flat on the other end, press it in a smaller hole in the wing, and glue or epoxy it in place at the final assembly.

11. <u>Cut the pivot tubing.</u> With a hacksaw, cut a one inch long piece of 3/8" OD copper tubing. With a file, deburr the edges.

12. <u>Drill the shaft hole.</u> When the glue has dried on the body, open up the ¼" hole through the wing bases and the body at the shaft location with a 9/32" diameter drill bit.

13. <u>Assemble and test the whirligig.</u> Now is a good time, before extensive carving has been done on the body and wings, to see how the whirligig will work.

Insert the 5/16 diameter stainless steel ball and the 1" length of 3/8" diameter copper tube into the pivot hole. Set the body on a whirligig stand or a spike in a vice. Insert the three ¾" long nylon bushings into the wing shaft hole.

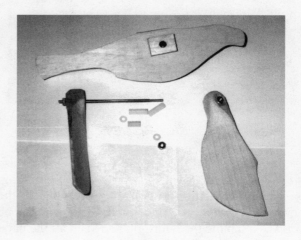

FIGURE 4.7

Screw the wing shaft into one of the wings and apply a brass washer and locking nut on the outside (*Figure 4.7*). Place a nylon washer on the shaft and insert it through the body and bushings. Place another nylon washer on the other side and screw on the other wing, allowing a loose, somewhat sloppy fit. Position the wings 180 degrees apart and put on the second washer and nut. Tighten both nuts and gently spin the shaft to check for alignment and balance.

This fine-tuning does not have to be very precise. Some mismatch is unavoidable, and whirligig wings are very forgiving. If the wings always end up in the same horizontal position, they are probably not aligned. Loosen the lock nut on one side, and rotate the wing slightly, then retighten. Repeat the process until the wings always stop in random positions.

If the same wing always stops on the bottom, it is probably heavier than the other, or has more material towards the wing tips. Remove the wing, compare it to the other wing, determine where some material may be removed, and adjust the shape accordingly. Reassemble and repeat this process if necessary.

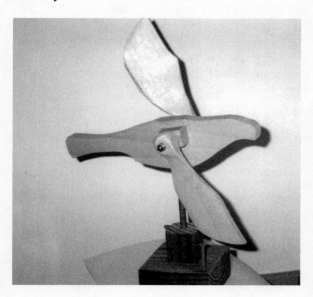

FIGURE 4.8

Now break out the fan and watch it go (*Figure 4.8*). You may discover more areas for fine tuning. Resist the temptation to call over everyone in the house to see what you've created – you're not done yet. Disassemble the whirligig and keep all the parts in one place.

14. Carve the body. Rough carve the eagle's body in high relief (*Figure 4.9*). Pay attention to the grain direction, and be careful not to make the bill and tail too delicate. To give a feeling of depth, the tail may be slanted from one side to the other. The downward point on the eagle's bill goes at right angles to the grain, so this area must be kept thicker than on a completely realistic carving. This does not distract from the finished appearance of the whirligig when it is mounted outside and flying in the breeze.

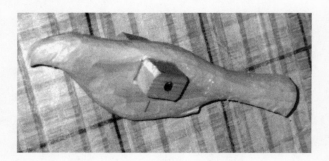

FIGURE 4.9

Finish carving the eagles body. The feet are tucked up into the lower part of the eagle's body, and don't require too much detail. The body may be sanded smooth, or the carving tool marks can be left visible. To increase the strength of delicate parts like the bill and the edge of the tail, these features may be soaked with super glue at this point.

FIGURE 4.10

15. Carve the wings. Finish carving the wings, with some thought given to the level of detail you want to add (*Figure 4.10*). Compare the shape of shoulder area with the body and wing bases to insure a smooth transition from wing to body. With

a pencil, sketch the primary and secondary feathers on both sides. With woodcarving tools – knives, gouges, skewed chisels and/or motorized carving bits - apply as much feather shape as you desire, being careful not to make the wing too delicate or to upset the balance between the wings. The wings may be left smooth and the feathers painted on. The wings will probably rotate better with the least amount of carving tool marks showing.

16. <u>Sand and prime.</u> If there are any rough edges on the body or wings, they should be lightly sanded now. Prime the body and wings with a good exterior primer. While being painted, the body can be mounted on a spike in the pivot hole, and the wings can be hung from copper wires, or pieces from an old wire coat hanger may be inserted in the shaft holes. When the primer dries, the wood grain will be rough and raised. Sand all over lightly with 220 very fine sand paper.

17. <u>Paint the parts.</u> Paint the wings and the main part of the body dark brown with gloss or high-gloss exterior enamel paint. The head will be white or bright white. The bill, feet and pupils of the eyes will be a bright yellow, such as sunflower yellow. The talons and center of the pupils will be black.

At least two coats will be required, with some colors – notably white, black and red (not needed here) for some reason covering much better than the others. Brown seems to require more coats.

18. <u>Final assembly.</u> When the paint dries, the whirligig can be reassembled (see step 13). Add lock washers or a drop of Loctite thread locker to the shaft on both sides for the lock nuts. Readjust the wings so that they spin freely and stop in random positions. Mount the eagle outside, and observe how it reacts to the wind.

Usually whirligigs require a break-in period of a few weeks. The wood will absorb moisture from the air and expand, or it may dry out a little. During this period, further adjustment may be required. The wings may bind up and refuse to spin. If the wings bind against the body, loosen the lock nut on one side and rotate the wing out one or two turns. If there seems to be clearance on the sides, but the shaft is stuck, this may be caused by the body swelling or warping slightly and constricting the shaft. Remove the shaft and bushings and open up the hole through the body with a slightly larger drill.

FIGURE 4.11

5

The Dragon Whirligig

FIGURE 5.1

Whirligig Dragons

Dragons have captured the imaginations of people of all ages and cultures for centuries or millennium. Whether inspired by dinosaur bones unearthed over the years, or by pure human fantasy, they have taken many forms and sizes. From beautiful oriental dragons who can be fierce or gentle with a ball in their claws, to medieval dragons, cartoon dragons, biblical serpents, Hollywood dragons, or celestial constellations (not to mention that punny, magical but illegal "drag- in", Puff), dragons are ideal subjects for whirligigs. Smaug from *The Hobbit* or Drago from the movie *Dragonheart* would be interesting models.

This dragon is more difficult to carve than the eagle, and requires some forethought. It is loosely based on a figure from a popular children's trading game. He (or she) is nine inches long and colored bright orange like the original with the inside of the wings hunter's green and the tail a fiery yellow and red. Other color schemes would work just as well, for example with a light green body.

The wings are shaped rather oddly, and because of their shape and size don't spin quite as freely as some of the other designs in this book. The dragon would rather laze in his cave with his treasure than fly off, and it takes him a little longer to get airborne. For better spinning, the wings can be made narrower and thinner, or even a little longer than the plan shows. The pattern may be stretched with a photocopier.

DRAGON PATTERN

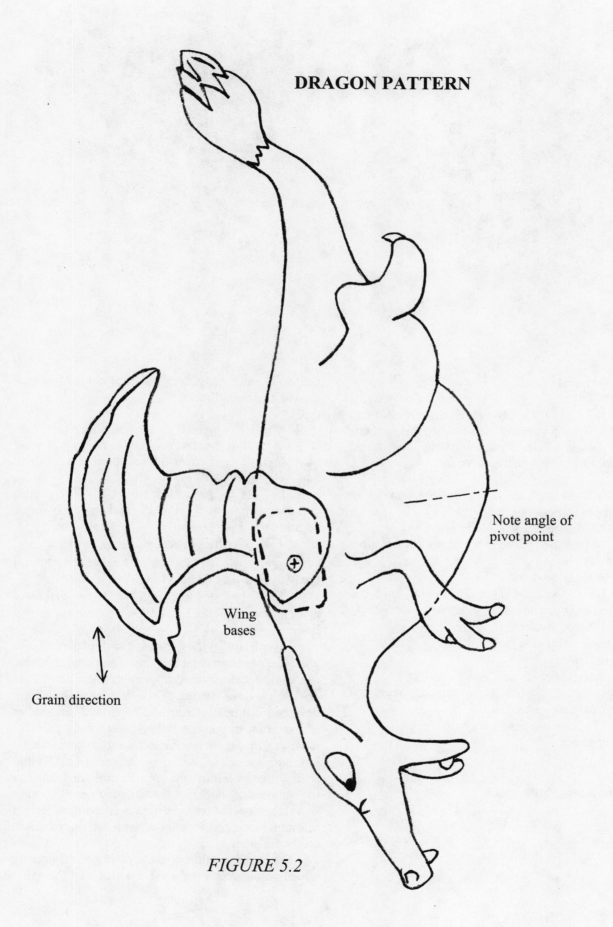

Note angle of
pivot point

Wing
bases

Grain direction

FIGURE 5.2

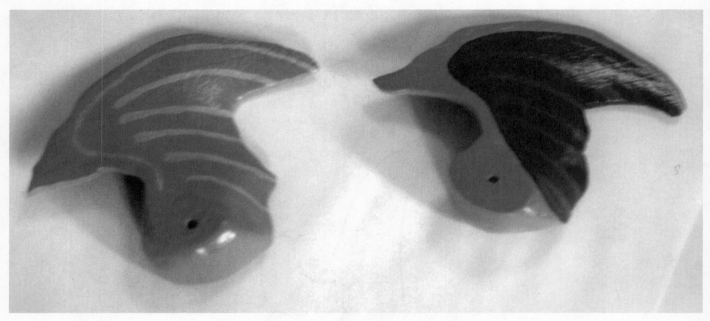

FIGURE 5.3

List of Material

This list includes all the materials necessary to make this dragon per the step-by-step instructions below. As with all the designs in this book, substitutions may be used as desired.

1. (1) 1" (3/4" actual) thick piece of seasoned or kiln dried pine wood, or equivalent
2. (1) 1/8" diameter x 4 ½" long brass rod
3. (1) 3/8 Outside Diameter x 1" long copper tube
4. (4) #6-32 brass nuts
5. (2) #6 brass washers
6. (3) .140 I.D x .250 O.D. x .75" long nylon tubes or bushings or equivalent lengths
7. (2) #6 nylon washers
8. Exterior wood glue
9. Loctite thread locker
10. Exterior primer
11. Bright orange, white, yellow, red, green and black exterior gloss paint
12. (1) 5/16 DIA stainless steel ball
13. Sandpaper

Dragon Step-by-Step

The basic steps and any particular construction techniques for making the dragon are listed here. The procedure is the same as for the eagle in

chapter 4, and more detailed information for each step will be found there.

1. Make a pattern. Photocopy or trace the plans *(Figure 5.2)* of the dragon's body, wings and wing bases on a sheet of paper or cardboard and cut them out.

2. Lay out the parts. Trace the body, two wings, and two wing bases on a 1" thick piece of pine, aligning the grain correctly.

3. Cut out the 5 pieces. Using a band saw, coping saw, jig saw, scroll saw or saber saw, cut out the body, 2 wings and 2 wing bases.

4. Mark hole locations on the body. Mark the pivot point, shaft and wing base locations on the body.

5. Mark the wings. Mark the location of the wing shaft hole on each of the wings and wing bases. Mark the shape of the wing's propeller blade on each of the wings. This dragon's wings are designed differently from the eagle and the soldier in this book in that the left and right wings are not identical. In *Figure 5.3* the left wing is shown on the left and the right wing is on the right. While both wings have the same profile and are shaped at the same angle, note that the outside of the left wing is rounded on the outside. The right wing is flat on that same side and is rounded with the thread insert on the far side.

The wings could be made identical, of course, which would create a different effect. For the eagle design, the front or leading edges of the wings are in line on both sides. So when one side is up, both leading edges are pointing forward, and when it's down, the trailing edges are pointing forward. For the dragon, when the left wing is up, it's facing forward and the right wing is backward and vice versa *(Figure 5.4)*.

FIGURE 5.4

Due to the intriguing shape of the dragon's wings, they will look fine whatever you prefer. Remember to plan ahead before cutting wood and to mark with pencil where material is to be removed and retained.

6. Drill the holes in the body. Drill the 3/8" by 1-1/8 " deep hole at the correct angle in the bottom of the body for the pivot point. Drill ¼" holes through the body and wing bases for the shaft.

7. Glue or screw the wing bases to the body.

8. Drill a hole for the shaft in the wing.   Drill a 3/32 diameter hole through the wings at the shaft location. If necessary for better locking, install a threaded insert or a nut in the wing.

9. Rough out the wings. With a pencil, label them "left" and "right" on the inside shoulder area. This will help you from getting confused as you carve the wing surfaces. Shape each wing into propeller vanes about 1/8" thick. Smooth the surfaces and round the outside of the shoulders.

10. Make the shaft. Make a shaft 4 1/2" long out of 1/8" diameter brass rod. Thread #6-32 for about 1/2 inch on each end.

11. Cut the pivot tubing. Cut a 1" long piece of 3/8" O. D. copper tubing for the pivot.

12. Drill the shaft hole. Drill 9/32 diameter through the body and wing bases at the shaft location.

13. Assemble the dragon and test it out. Fine tune the wings so that they are in balance, spin freely and stop in random positions. Disassemble and save the parts.

14. Carve the body. Carve the dragon's body in high relief adding as much detail as desired.

15. Carve the wings. Finish carving the wings and sand smooth.

16. Prime and sand. Prime the body and wings with a good exterior primer. When the primer is dry, sand lightly with fine sand paper.

17. Paint the parts. Paint the wings and body with a high gloss exterior enamel paint. The outside of the wings and the body is orange. The inside of the wings is dark green. The flame on the tail is yellow with bright red on the end. The stomach, eyes, teeth, and claws are white. The tongue and inside of the mouth are red. Of course, any number of color schemes will work with a dragon.

18. Final assembly. Reassemble the whirligig and add loctite or lock washers to the shaft. Readjust the wings so that they spin freely and stop in random positions. Mount the dragon outside and allow it to become acclimated to the weather, adjusting and tweaking the wings as necessary.

6

The Knight Whirligig

FIGURE 6.1

The Arm-Waving Knight

Having set an unruly dragon loose, we must protect ourselves with a knight. This design is based on an actual suit of armor displayed at the Higgins Armory Museum in Worcester, Massachusetts.

Unlike the eagle and dragon whirligigs that are carved in high relief, the knight whirligig is a fully shaped, in-the-round woodcarving. The knight is mounted on a base, with a tail shaped like a shield. This insures the knight is oriented correctly with the wind, and the arms with swords always rotate in the desired direction. This base may be omitted, but then the pivot point may need to be relocated a little, and the performance may be a bit erratic.

Knight whirligigs are intriguing because of the variety of weapons available. This Knight has a sword in each hand, but he would be fun to make with maces, axes, spears, flails, hammers, or a combination of weapons. If a different weapon is used for each arm, some thought must be given to their shape. Ideally, the finished arms should weigh about the same and be balanced so they spin evenly and easily, and come to a stop in random positions.

For the simplest finish, the knight only requires silver paint. If more color is desired, a bright plume, a tunic or a cape may be added to the pattern before carving.

The pattern (*Figure 6.2*) is sized for a 2 ¼ inch square (actual size) by 8 ¼ inch long piece of wood. It may be rescaled up or down to fit your available wood stock. As an alternative, the 2 ¼ inch thickness is easy to obtain with a one inch finished pine board. This is actually ¾ inch thick, so gluing and clamping three pieces together gives the 2 ¼ inch thickness.

KNIGHT PATTERN

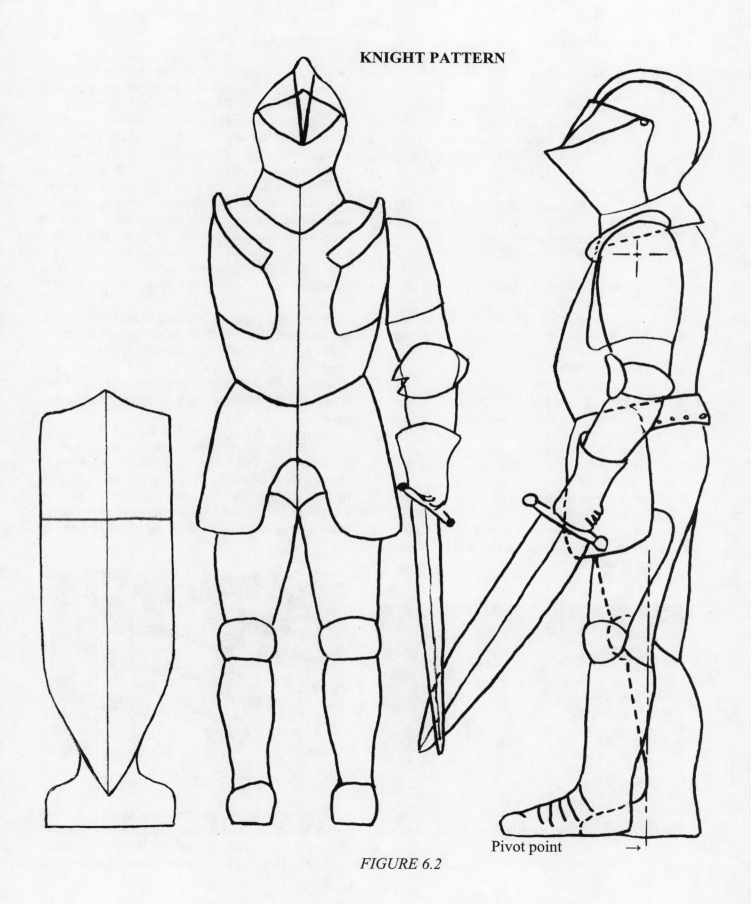

Pivot point

FIGURE 6.2

27

List of Material

This list includes all the material necessary to make this knight whirligig by the book. The function of all these items will be described in the step-by-step instructions. Alternate material can be used in most cases. The shaft, for example, could be a wood dowel, glued into the arms and riding in a bushing made from a copper tube.

1. (1) 2.25 x 2.25 x 8.25" (actual size) piece of seasoned or kiln-dried pine wood, or equivalent, for the knight's body
2. (1) piece of 1" (.75 actual) pine board for the arms
3. (1) piece of .25" x 1.5" x 12" pine board for the base and shield
4. (1) 1/8" diameter x 3 ¼ " long brass rod
5. (1) 3/8 Outside Diameter x 4 ½ " long copper tube
6. (4) #6-32 brass nuts
7. (2) #6 brass washers
8. (3) .140 I.D x .250 O.D. x .625" long (or equivalent) nylon tube or bushings
9. (2) #6 nylon washers
10. (1) wood screw, brass or stainless steel
11. Sand paper – 130 and 220 grit or equivalent
12. Exterior wood glue
13. Loctite thread locker
14. Exterior primer
15. Silver (or aluminum), gray, red, blue and green (or any other colors that you think would be fitting) exterior gloss paint
16. (1) 5/16 DIA stainless steel ball

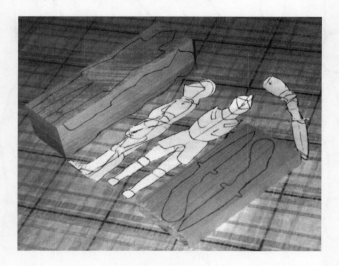

FIGURE 6.3

The Knight Step-by-Step

1. <u>Make a pattern.</u> Photocopy or trace the plans *(Figure 6.2)* on cardboard or paper for the side view, front view and arms, and cut them out.

2. <u>Lay out the parts.</u> Trace the pattern shape of the knight's front view on a 2.25 inch thick block of wood (*Figure 6.3*). If necessary, three pieces of one inch finished wood can be laminated to obtain the 2.25 inch thickness. Trace the side view on the side of the block making sure the features are aligned at the same height as the front view. Mark the spot for the shaft hole in the shoulder. Mark the spot on the bottom for the pivot hole. Trace the arms on a 1" (3/4" actual) piece of wood , making sure the grain runs the length of the sword. Mark the spot for the shaft hole.

3. <u>Drill the holes in the body.</u> It's usually easier to locate and align the shaft and pivot hole correctly at this point. Put the block on the drill press, or use a hand drill and add the 9/32" hole through the shoulder for the shaft and bushings. Then drill the 3/8 hole in the bottom about 4- ½ inches deep for the pivot tube.

4. <u>Cut out the 3 pieces.</u> Cut out the front view with a band saw, jig saw or coping saw. To save time removing material from the body, temporarily reattach the sawed-off pieces with a couple of small nails or a couple spots of super glue and cut out the side view with a band saw. Cut out the two arms from a one-inch board with a jig, band or coping saw.

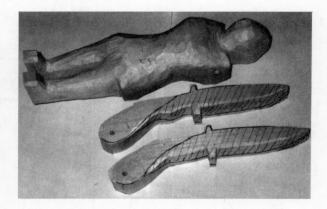

FIGURE 6.4

5. <u>Mark the arms.</u> Sketch the shape of the propeller blade on each arm. Both arms should be shaped the same except for the shoulders, which should be rounded on opposite sides. If both arms

were identical, one would appear to be bent the wrong way at the elbow when assembled.

If you prefer the arms to rotate forward over the top (which seems most logical), and if you have a preference for which way the knight faces into your prevailing winds, you should give some thought to the "pitch" of the arm propeller blades. While both arms will be shaped the same (except for the shoulders), if the blades are slanted the opposite way, the arms will rotate in the opposite direction.

If your knight is to be mounted with another whirligig, such as a dragon, the arms/swords may be designed so that the knight is always facing and fighting the dragon in your prevailing winds.

6. Drill the shaft hole in the arms. Drill a 3/32" hole through the arms at the shaft location. If conventional threaded inserts are to be used in the arms, drill the pilot hole in the outside of the shoulder area. To use a nut for an insert, drill a 9/32" hole about 1/8" deep. Screw a #6-32 threaded shaft (if one is not available, see step 8) through the arm as a guide, so that it extends slightly beyond the outside surface. Screw the nut on the shaft and carefully hammer the nut into the 9/32" hole until it is flush with the surface. Remove the shaft.

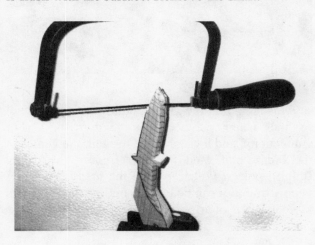

FIGURE 6.5

7. Rough carve the arms. Using a band saw, coping saw, jig saw, chisels, knives and/or gouges, carefully remove the material from both sides of the arms to make a propeller vane about 1/8" thick *(Figure 6.5)*. With a knife, round off the outside of the shoulders. At this point, both arms should be relatively smooth and very close in size, shape and weight. Carving of armor detail should wait until after the arms are tested in step 11.

8. Make the shaft. With a hacksaw, cut a 3 ¼ " long piece of 1/8" diameter brass rod. Using a file, round off and deburr the edges. Thread each end about ½ inch long with a #6-32 die *(Figure 2.3)*. One way to do this is to clamp the rod in the middle with vice-grip pliers, and set the vice-grips on a vice for further stability. Apply some cutting fluid to the rod and die, and carefully screw the die down the rod, backing off once in a while, being careful not to bend the shaft. Unscrew the die, flip the vice-grips over and repeat for the other side. Remove the vice-grips and lightly sand any indentations they may have made in the shaft.

As an alternative, make the shaft slightly shorter and thread only one end. File a flat on the other end, press it in a smaller hole in the arm, and glue or epoxy it in place at the final assembly.

9. Cut the pivot tubing. With a hacksaw, cut a 4-½ inch long piece of 3/8" OD copper tubing. With a file, deburr the edges.

10. Cut out the base and the tail. Most likely you will want to mount the knight on a base board with some sort of a tail to insure the arms always face into the wind and rotate forward over the top. If you are not sure which way to proceed, you might want to hold off on this step and see how the whirligig behaves without the base, in which case proceed to step 11.

The base is a thin piece of wood about 8 inches long or longer, on which the knight stands. In this design, a shield is placed on the other end to act as the vane or tail to cause the knight's arms to swing into the wind. Instead of a shield, a silhouette of a castle, or of the knight's faithful steed, or pennants from the jousting tilt may be used.

11. Assemble and test the whirligig. It is probably a good idea at some point, before extensive carving has been done on the body and arms, to see how the whirligig will work. For testing, the arms should be close to their final shape, but it doesn't matter if the body is rough carved, or right off the band saw.

Insert the 5/16 diameter stainless steel ball and the 4 ½ " length of 3/8" diameter copper tube into the pivot hole. Set the body on a whirligig stand or a spike in a vice. Insert the three 5/8" long nylon bushings into the arm shaft hole.

Screw the arm shaft into one of the arms and apply a locking nut on the outside *(Figure 6.6)*. Place a nylon washer on the shaft and insert it through the body and bushings. Place another nylon washer on the other side and screw on the other arm, allowing a loose, somewhat sloppy fit. Position the arms 180 degrees apart and put on a locking nut. Tighten both nuts and gently spin the shaft to check for alignment and balance.

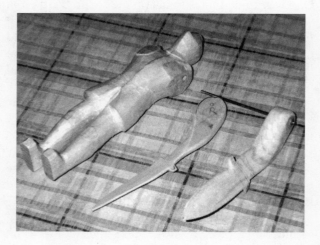

FIGURE 6.6

This fine-tuning does not have to be very precise. Some mismatch is unavoidable, and whirligig arms can be very forgiving. If the arms always end up in the same horizontal position, they are probably not aligned properly. Instead of a theoretical straight line going through the center of gravity of both arms, the actual configuration of the arms may resemble an upside down "V". Loosen the lock nut on one side, rotate one arm up slightly, and then retighten. Repeat the process until the arms always stop in random positions.

If the same arm always stops on the bottom, it is probably heavier than the other arm, or has more material towards the end of the sword. Remove the arm, compare it to the other arm, determine where some material may be removed, and carve off enough to adjust the shape accordingly. Reassemble and repeat this process if necessary

Set up a fan and see how the whirligig behaves. You may decide at this time that the knight whirls and gigs quite well without any tail. If, however, you intend to mount the knight on a base with a shield or some other object for a tail, verify which side to place the tail so that the arms always rotate forward. Position the knight on the base and sketch a line for reference around the feet. Drill a 3/8 inch hole through the base for the pivot hole tube. Drill a pilot hole through the base and into one of the knight's feet for a screw that will help hold everything together at the final assembly. Assemble the shield, or whatever you are using for a tail, to the base with glue or screws.

You may discover more areas for fine-tuning. When you are satisfied with the performance of the arms/swords, disassemble the whirligig and keep all the parts in one place.

12. <u>Carve the body.</u> This knight went through two stages of rough carving. The first, raw carving of the body *(Figure 6.4)* removed unnecessary wood and rounded it off. Remember to draw a centerline with a pencil from front to back on the torso, and through the front and back of the knight's legs. If parts of these lines are carved away, redraw the section before too long. Do a secondary roughing of the knight's body to bring it closer to the final shape, being careful not to remove any final features *(Figure 6.7)*.

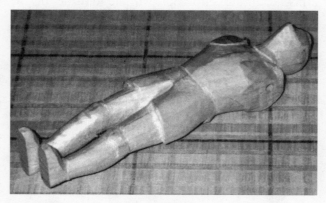

FIGURE 6.7

Finish carving the knight, adding as much detail of the armor as necessary *(Figure 6.9)*. For authenticity, add a crest shape through the center of the breast plate and the leg armor – the cuisse (thigh), poleyn (kneecap) and the greave (shin). A vee parting tool can be used to outline the visor and various layers of armor.

FIGURE 6.8

grain, so they should be left a little larger than desirable in a completely realistic woodcarving. The shoulders are wider than normal so that the swords don't rub against the armor skirt (fauld and tasset). The top of the arms are larger at the shoulder joint for strength.

Unlike many of the other whirligigs in this book, this one should be sanded smooth instead of left with tool marks. To save time sanding, additional fine cuts can be made with the knife to make the surface as smooth as possible. Some of the finish shape and detail on the helmet can be added by sanding.

13. <u>Finish carving the arms.</u> With a pencil, sketch the location of the various parts of armor on the arms. The plate armor at the elbow is called the couter. The metal gloves are gauntlets. Undercut the edges of these features to give the impression of depth to the joints, and carve the fingers in the hand and the hilt of the sword, being careful not to weaken or adversely affect the aerodynamics of the arm/sword. Before sanding and painting, you might want to reassemble the whirligig for one last test *(Figure 6.10)*.

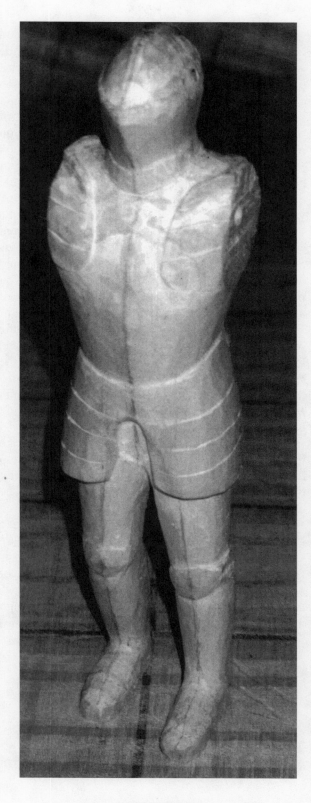

FIGURE 6.9

Certain parts of the knight will be beefed up to survive outdoors without detracting from the overall effect. The feet are at right angles to the wood's

FIGURE 6.10

14. <u>Sand and prime.</u> Rough sand the body and arms/swords with a medium grade sand paper – around 130 grit. Anything coarser might leave scratch marks which would require additional

sanding to remove. Do a finish sanding with 220 grit paper *(Figure 6.11)*.

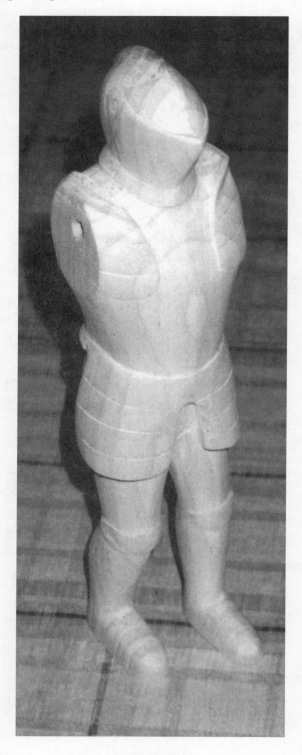

FIGURE 6.11

15. <u>Paint the parts.</u> Apply the first coat of a good exterior primer. When it is dry, the grain of the wood will be raised. Sand all over with a 220 grit paper and apply the second coat of primer and allow it to dry.

Apply the finish coats of paint. The exact color of polished steel is difficult to duplicate, so you may have to be creative. The knight will look impressive with the armor covered with silver, or perhaps aluminum, paint. I have only found these exterior metallic paints in oil base, but they cover well with just one coat. The portions of the knight's body that are not protected by armor can be painted some other color, such as gray. The knight stands on a green base board. The shield should be painted in bright colors such as red and blue. You might want to put your name or your own coat of arms on the shield.

16. <u>Final assembly.</u> When the paint dries, the whirligig can be reassembled (see step 11). Add lock washers or a drop of Loctite thread locker to the shaft on both sides for the insert and lock nuts. Readjust the arms so that they spin freely and stop in random positions. Mount the knight outside, and observe how it reacts to the wind.

Usually whirligigs require a break-in period of a few weeks. The wood will absorb moisture from the air and expand, or it may dry out a little. During this period, further adjustment may be required. The arms may bind up and refuse to spin. If the arms bind against the body, loosen the lock nut on one side and rotate the arm out one or two turns. If there seems to be clearance on the sides, but the shaft is stuck, this may be caused by the body swelling or warping slightly and constricting the shaft. Remove the shaft and bushings and open up the hole through the body with a slightly larger drill. Sometimes final adjustments might be needed after a couple of weeks.

7

Major Pitcairn Whirligig

FIGURE 7.1

Historical Background

Soldiers have always been popular subjects for whirligigs. The colorful uniforms of the eighteenth and nineteenth centuries make for interesting designs. The subject of this whirligig comes from the American Revolution where the uniforms of the different countries and colonies shared many similarities. While accuracy down to the smallest detail is not necessary, this whirligig is based on an historic figure and the design shown here is based on the recorded descriptions of his uniform. Different period soldiers can be made from the same pattern by changing the color of the coat, or the style of hat.

It can be argued that Major John Pitcairn of the Royal Marines started the American Revolutionary War. On the morning of April 19, 1775, Colonel Francis Smith was lagging behind with the main body of the British army while Major Pitcairn was in command of the lead elements that approached Lexington Green and the waiting American minutemen. Pitcairn rode up to Captain John Parker

of the Lexington militia and ordered the rebels to disperse. Some unknown person fired a shot, and the British responded with a volley, indiscriminate fire, and a bayonet charge that sent the outnumbered Colonials retreating. The fighting had begun.

Major Pitcairn was well liked and respected by the leading men on both sides of the conflict. His steadiness and leadership on that spring morning helped the badgered British column survive its retreat from Concord to Boston after "the shot heard round the world." Two months later with his son present, he paid the ultimate price of the war when he died from his wounds at the battle of Bunker Hill.

Due to his role (on the wrong side) in the struggle for America's freedom and independence, Major Pitcairn is a suitable subject for a whirligig. He wears the uniform of the British Royal Marines, with an officer's gorget at his throat and a sash around his waist, a red coat and white breaches with black riding boots.

SOLDIER PATTERN

FIGURE 7.2

LEXINGTON

Pivot point

FIGURE 7.3

List of Material

This list includes all the material necessary to make this soldier whirligig by the book. The function of all these items will be described in the step-by-step instructions. Alternate material can be used in most cases. The shaft, for example, could be a wood dowel, glued into the arms and riding in a bushing made from a copper tube.

1. (1) 2 x 1.75 x 9" (actual size) piece of seasoned or kiln dried pine wood, or equivalent, for the soldier's body
2. (1) piece of 1" (.75" actual) pine board for the arms
3. (1) piece of .25 x 1.5 x 12" pine board for the base and mile marker
4. (1) 1/8" diameter x 3 ½ " long brass rod
5. (1) 3/8 Outside Diameter x 4" long copper tube
6. (4) #6-32 brass nuts
7. (2) #6 brass washers
8. (3) .140 I.D x .250 O.D. x .62" long nylon tubes or bushings
9. (2) #6 nylon washers
10. (1) wood screw, brass or stainless steel
11. (1) 5/16 DIA stainless steel ball
12. Sand paper – 130 and 220 grit or equivalent
13. Exterior wood glue
14. Loctite thread locker
15. Exterior primer
16. Red, white, blue, black, green and silver (or any other colors that you think would be fitting) exterior gloss paint

The Soldier Step-by-Step

The basic steps and any particular construction techniques for making the soldier are listed here. The procedure is the same as for the knight shown in Chapter 6, and more detailed information for each step will be found there.

1. Make a pattern. Photocopy or trace the plans *(Figure 7.2)* on cardboard or paper for the side view, front view and arms, and cut them out.

2. Lay out the parts. Trace the pattern shape of the soldier's front view on a 2" block of wood. Trace the side view on the side of the block making sure the features are aligned at the same height as the front view. Mark the spot for the shaft hole in the shoulder. Mark the spot on the bottom for the pivot hole. Trace the arms on a 1" piece of wood, making sure the grain runs the length of the sword. Mark the spot for the shaft hole.

3. Drill the holes in the body. It's usually easier to locate and align the shaft and pivot hole correctly at this point. Put the block on the drill press, or use a hand drill and add the 9/32 hole through the shoulder for the shaft and bushings. Then add the 3/8 hole in the bottom for the pivot tube.

4. Cut out the pieces. Cut out the front view with a band saw, coping saw or jig saw. To save time removing material from the body, temporarily reattach the sawed-off pieces with a couple of small nails or a couple of drops of super glue and cut out the side view. Cut out the two arms.

5. Mark the arms. Sketch the shape of the arm's propeller blade on each arm. Both arms should be shaped the same.

If you prefer the arms to rotate forward over the top (which seems most logical), and if you have a preference for which way the soldier faces into your prevailing winds, you should give some thought to the "pitch" of the arm propeller blades. While both arms will be shaped the same, if the blades are slanted the opposite way, the arms will rotate in the opposite direction.

6. Drill the shaft hole in the arms. Drill a 3/32" hole through the arms at the shaft location. If conventional threaded inserts are to be used in the arms, drill the pilot hole in the outside of the shoulder area. To use a nut for an insert, drill a 9/32" hole about 1/8" deep. Screw a #6-32 threaded shaft (if one is not available, see step 8) through the arm as a guide, so that it extends slightly beyond the outside surface. Screw the nut on the shaft and

carefully hammer the nut into the 9/32" hole until it is flush with the surface. Remove the shaft.

7. <u>Rough carve the arms.</u> Using a band saw, coping saw, jig saw, chisels, knives and/or gouges, carefully remove the material from both sides of the arms to make a propeller vane about 1/8" thick. With a knife, round off the outside of the shoulders. At this point, both arms should be relatively smooth and very close in size, shape and weight. Carving of more detail should wait until after the arms are tested in step 11.

FIGURE 7.4

8. <u>Make the shaft.</u> With a hacksaw, cut a 3 ½ " long piece of 1/8" diameter brass rod. Using a file, round off and deburr the edges. Thread each end about ½ inch long with a #6-32 die. One way to do this is to clamp the rod in the middle with vice-grip pliers, and set the vice-grips on a vice for further stability. Apply some cutting fluid to the rod and die, and carefully screw the die down the rod, backing off once in a while, being careful not to bend the shaft. Unscrew the die, flip the vice-grips over and repeat for the other side. Remove the vice-grips and lightly sand any indentations they may have made in the shaft.

9. <u>Cut the pivot tubing.</u> With a hacksaw, cut a four-inch long piece of 3/8" OD copper tubing. With a file, deburr the edges.

10. <u>Cut out the base and the tail.</u> Most likely you will want to mount the soldier on a base board with some sort of a tail to insure the arms always face into the wind and rotate forward over the top. You might want to hold off on this step and see how the whirligig behaves without the base, in which case proceed to step 11.

The base is a thin piece of wood about 10 inches long or longer, which the soldier stands on. In this design a stone marker is placed on the other end to act as the vane or tail to cause the soldier's arms to swing into the wind. The marker has "Lexington" on one side and "Concord" on the other.

11. <u>Assemble and test the whirligig.</u> It is probably a good idea at some point, before extensive carving has been done on the body and arms, to see how the whirligig will work. For testing, the arms should be close to their final shape, but it doesn't matter if the body is rough-carved, or right off the band saw.

Insert the 5/16 diameter stainless steel ball and the 4" length of 3/8" diameter copper tube into the pivot hole. Set the body on a whirligig stand or a spike in a vice. Insert the three 5/8" long nylon bushings into the arm shaft hole.

Screw the arm shaft into one of the arms and apply a locking nut on the outside. Place a nylon washer on the shaft and insert it through the body and bushings. Place another nylon washer on the other side and screw on the other arm, allowing a loose, somewhat sloppy, fit. Position the arms 180 degrees apart and put on a locking nut. Tighten both nuts and gently spin the shaft to check for alignment and balance.

This fine tuning does not have to be very precise. Some mismatch is unavoidable, and whirligig arms can be very forgiving. If the arms always end up in the same horizontal position, they are probably not aligned properly. Instead of a theoretical straight line going through the center of gravity of both arms, the actual configuration of the arms may resemble an upside down "V". Loosen the lock nut on one side, rotate one arm up slightly, and then retighten. Repeat the process until the arms always stop in random positions.

If the same arm always stops on the bottom, it is probably heavier than the other arm, or has more material towards the end of the sword. Remove the arm, compare it to the other arm, determine where some material may be removed, and carve off enough to adjust the shape accordingly. Reassemble and repeat this process if necessary.

Set up a fan and see how the whirligig behaves. You may decide at this time that the soldier whirls and gigs quite well without any tail. If, however, you intend to mount the whirligig on a base with a mile marker or some other object for a tail, verify which side to place the tail so that the arms always rotate forward. Position the soldier on the base and sketch a line for reference around the feet. Drill a 3/8 inch hole through the base for the pivot hole tube. Drill a pilot hole through the base and into one of the soldier's feet for a screw that will help hold everything together at the final assembly. Attach the mile marker to the base with glue or screws.

You may discover more areas for fine-tuning. When you are satisfied with the performance of the arms/swords, disassemble the whirligig and keep all the parts in one place.

12. <u>Carve the body.</u> This soldier went through two stages of rough carving. The first, raw carving of the body removed unnecessary wood and rounded it off. Remember to draw a centerline with a pencil from front to back on the torso, and through the front and back of the soldier's legs. If parts of these lines are carved away, redraw the section before too long. Do a secondary roughing of the soldier's body to bring it closer to the final shape, being careful not to remove any final features.

Finish carving the soldier, adding as much detail of the uniform as necessary. Certain parts of the soldier will be beefed up to survive outdoors without detracting from the overall effect. The feet are at right angles to the wood's grain, so they should be left a little larger than desirable in a completely realistic woodcarving. The shoulders are wider than normal so that the swords don't rub against the body. The top of the arms are larger at the shoulder joint for strength.

13. <u>Finish carving the arms.</u> With a pencil, sketch the location of the various parts of the uniform on the arms. Undercut the edges of these features to give the impression of depth to the joints, being careful not to weaken or adversely affect the aerodynamics of the arm/sword. Before sanding and painting, you might want to reassemble the whirligig for one last test.

14. <u>Sand and prime.</u> Rough sand the swords with a medium grade sand paper – around 130 grit. Anything coarser might leave scratch marks which would require additional sanding to remove. Do a finish sanding with 220 grit paper.

15. <u>Paint the parts.</u> Apply the first coat of a good exterior primer. When it is dry, the grain of the wood will be raised. Lightly sand all over with a 220 grit paper and apply the second coat of primer and allow it to dry.

Apply the finish coats of paint. The soldier's coat is red with white or blue lapels, the pants and straps are white, the boots and hat are black, the gorget is gold, silver or yellow and the sash is blue. The face and hands are flesh colored, made with white paint with a drop of red to get the right tone. The base is green and the mile marker is gray.

FIGURE 7.5

16. <u>Final assembly</u> When the paint dries, the whirligig can be reassembled (see step 11). Add lock washers or a drop of Loctite thread locker to the shaft on both sides for the insert and lock nuts. Readjust the arms so that they spin freely and stop in random positions. Mount the soldier outside, and observe how it reacts to the wind.

Usually whirligigs require a break-in period of a few weeks. The wood will absorb moisture from the air and expand, or it may dry out a little. During this period, further adjustment may be required. The arms may bind up and refuse to spin. If the arms bind against the body, loosen the lock nut on one side and rotate the arm out one or two turns. If there seems to be clearance on the sides, but the shaft is stuck, this may be caused by the body swelling or warping slightly and constricting the shaft. Remove the shaft and bushings and open up the hole through the body with a slightly larger drill. Sometimes final adjustments might be needed after a couple of weeks.

8

The Boxer Whirligig

FIGURE 8.1

Notes on the Design

I wish I had thought of it, but this was my Uncle Bob's idea. His instructions to me were simple: "You make whirligigs. I need a gift for a friend of mine, "Iron" Mike Pusateri, who is a retired professional boxer. A boxer, with his arms spinning, is the perfect subject for a whirligig. Make me a boxer whirligig." As usual, he was right.

The design almost came together by itself. The boxer's muscular shoulders provide clearance for his arms to rotate freely. His broad arms make excellent propellers without being overly long. He is mounted on a base colored blue like the floor of a canvas ring.

The tail has a natural wood finish, holding a mallet and a gong with the boxer's name. This tail insures the boxer's arms are always rotating forward over the top. If desired, the boxer may be mounted on his pivot point without this base and tail, which would allow him to get in some uppercuts when the wind reverses.

This boxer is Caucasian, but with little or no adjustment he could easily be African American or from any ethnic group.

BOXER PATTERN

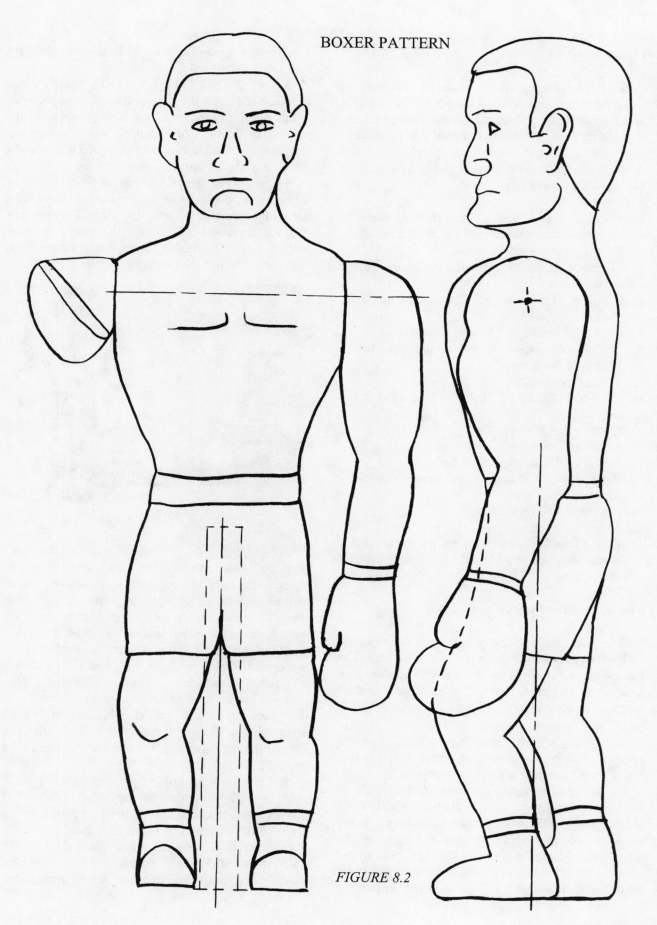

FIGURE 8.2

39

List of Material

This list includes all the material necessary to make this boxer whirligig by the book. The function of all these items will be described in the step-by-step instructions. Alternate material can be used in most cases. The shaft, for example, could be a wood dowel, glued into the arms and riding in a bushing made from a copper tube.

1. (1) 2 x 2 ½ x 9 ¼ " (actual size) piece of seasoned or kiln dried pine wood, or equivalent, for the boxers body
2. (1) piece of 1" (.75 actual) pine board for the arms
3. (1) piece of .25 x 1.5 x 12" long pine board for the base and tail
4. (1) 1/8" diameter x 4.5" long brass rod
5. (1) 3/8 outside diameter x 4" long copper tube
6. (4) #6-32 brass nuts
7. (2) #6 brass washers
8. (3) .140 I.D x .250 O.D. x .75" long nylon tubes or bushings
9. (2) #6 nylon washers
10. (1) wood screw, brass or stainless steel
11. (1) 5/16 DIA stainless steel ball
12. Sand paper – 130 and 220 grit or equivalent
13. Exterior wood glue
14. Loctite thread locker
15. Exterior primer
16. Red, white, blue, black, or brown (or any other colors that you think would be fitting) exterior gloss paint

The Boxer Step by Step

The basic steps and any particular construction techniques for making the boxer are listed here. The procedure is the same as for the knight shown in Chapter 6, and more detailed information for each step will be found there.

1. Make a pattern. Photocopy or trace the plans *(Figure 8.2)* on cardboard or paper for the side view, front view and arms. Cut them out.
2. Lay out the parts. Trace the pattern shape of the boxer's front view on a 2" block of wood. Trace the side view on the side of the block making sure the features are aligned at the same height as the front view. Mark the spot for the shaft hole in the shoulder. Mark the spot on the bottom for the pivot hole. Trace the arms on a 1" piece of wood , making

sure the grain runs the length of the arm. Mark the spot for the shaft hole.

3. Drill the holes in the body. It's usually easier to locate and align the shaft and pivot hole correctly at this point. Put the block on the drill press, or use a hand drill and add the 9/32 hole through the shoulder for the shaft and bushings. Then add the 3/8 hole in the bottom for the pivot tube.

4. Cut out the pieces. Cut out the front view with a band saw, coping saw or jig saw. To save time removing material from the body, temporarily reattach the sawed-off pieces with a couple of small nails or a couple spots of super glue and cut out the side view. Cut out the two arms.

FIGURE 8.3

5. Mark the arms. Sketch the shape of the arm's propeller blade on each arm. Both arms should be shaped the same except for the shoulders, which should be rounded on opposite sides. If both arms were identical, one would appear to be bent the wrong way at the elbow when assembled.

If you prefer the arms to rotate forward over the top (which seems most logical), and if you have a preference for which way the boxer faces into your prevailing winds, you should give some thought to the "pitch" of the arm propeller blades. While both arms will be shaped the same, if the blades are slanted the opposite way, the arms will rotate in the opposite direction.

6. Drill the shaft hole in the arms. Drill a 3/32" hole through the arms at the shaft location. If conventional threaded inserts are to be used in the arms, drill the pilot hole in the outside of the shoulder area. To use a nut for an insert, drill a 9/32" hole about 1/8" deep. Screw a #6-32 threaded shaft (if one is not available, see step 8) through the

arm as a guide, so that it extends slightly beyond the outside surface. Screw the nut on the shaft and carefully hammer the nut into the 9/32" hole until it is flush with the surface. Remove the shaft.

7. <u>Rough carve the arms.</u> Using a band saw, coping saw, jig saw, chisels, knives and/or gouges, carefully remove the material from both sides of the arms to make a propeller vane about 1/8" thick. With a knife, round off the outside of the shoulders. At this point, both arms should be relatively smooth and very close in size, shape and weight. Carving of more detail should wait until after the arms are tested in step 11.

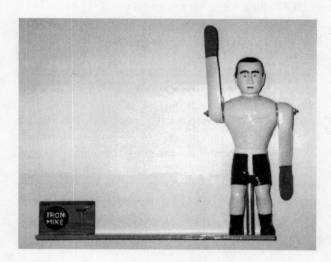

FIGURE 8.4

8. <u>Make the shaft.</u> With a hacksaw, cut a 4 ½ " long piece of 1/8" diameter brass rod. Using a file, round off and deburr the edges. Thread each end about ½ inch long with a #6-32 die (*Figure 2.3*). One way to do this is to clamp the rod in the middle with vice-grip pliers, and set the vice-grips on a vice for further stability. Apply some cutting fluid to the rod and die, and carefully screw the die down the rod, backing off once in a while, being careful not to bend the shaft. Unscrew the die, flip the vice-grips over and repeat for the other side. Remove the vice-grips and lightly sand any indentations they may have made in the shaft.

9. <u>Cut the pivot tubing.</u> With a hacksaw, cut a four-inch long piece of 3/8" OD copper tubing. With a file, deburr the edges.

10. <u>Cut out the base and the tail.</u> Most likely you will want to mount the boxer on a base board with some sort of a tail to insure the arms always face into the wind and rotate forward over the top. You might want to hold off on this step and see how the whirligig behaves without the base, in which case proceed to step 11.

The base is a thin piece of wood about 10 inches long or longer, which the boxer stands on. In this design a gong is placed on the other end to act as the vane or tail to cause the boxer's arms to swing into the wind.

11. <u>Assemble and test the whirligig.</u> It is probably a good idea at some point, before extensive carving has been done on the body and arms, to see how the whirligig will work. For testing, the arms should be close to their final shape, but it doesn't matter if the body is rough carved, or right off the band saw.

Insert the 5/16 diameter stainless steel ball and the 4" length of 3/8" diameter copper tube into the pivot hole. Set the body on a whirligig stand or a spike in a vice. Insert the three ¾" long nylon bushings into the arm shaft hole.

Screw the arm shaft into one of the arms and apply a locking nut on the outside. Place a nylon washer on the shaft and insert it through the body and bushings. Place another nylon washer on the other side and screw on the other arm, allowing a loose, somewhat sloppy, fit. Position the arms 180 degrees apart and put on a locking nut. Tighten both nuts and gently spin the shaft to check for alignment and balance.

This fine tuning does not have to be very precise. Some mismatch is unavoidable, and whirligig arms can be very forgiving. If the arms always end up in the same horizontal position, they are probably not aligned properly. Instead of a theoretical straight line going through the center of gravity of both arms, the actual configuration of the arms may resemble an upside down "V". Loosen the lock nut on one side, rotate one arm up slightly, and then retighten. Repeat the process until the arms always stop in random positions.

If the same arm always stops on the bottom, it is probably heavier than the other arm, or has more material towards the end of the boxing glove. Remove the arm, compare it to the other arm, determine where some material may be removed, and carve off enough to adjust the shape accordingly. Reassemble and repeat this process if necessary

Set up a fan and see how the whirligig behaves. You may decide at this time that the boxer whirls and gigs quite well without any tail. If, however, you intend to mount the whirligig on a base with a

41

gong or some other object for a tail, verify which side to place the tail so that the arms always rotate forward. Position the boxer on the base and sketch a line for reference around the feet. Drill a 3/8 inch hole through the base for the pivot hole tube. Drill a pilot hole through the base and into one of the boxer's feet for a screw that will help hold everything together at the final assembly.

You may discover more areas for fine tuning. When you are satisfied with the performance of the arms, disassemble the whirligig and keep all the parts in one place.

12. <u>Carve the body.</u> This boxer went through two stages of rough carving. The first, raw carving of the body removed unnecessary wood and rounded it off. Remember to draw a centerline with a pencil from front to back on the torso, and through the front and back of the boxer's legs. If parts of these lines are carved away, redraw the section before too long. Do a secondary roughing of the boxer's body to bring it closer to the final shape, being careful not to remove any final features.

Finish carving the boxer, adding as much body detail as necessary. Certain parts of the boxer will be beefed up to survive outdoors without detracting from overall the effect. The feet are at right angles to the wood's grain, so they should be left a little larger than desirable in a completely realistic woodcarving. The shoulders are wider than normal so that the arms don't rub against the body. The top of the arms are larger at the shoulder joint for strength.

13. <u>Finish carving the arms.</u> With a pencil, sketch the muscles and gloves on the arms. Undercut the edges of these features to give the impression of depth to the joints, and carve the gloves, being careful not to weaken or adversely affect the aerodynamics of the arm. Before sanding and painting, you might want to reassemble the whirligig for one last test.

14. <u>Sand and prime.</u> Rough sand the arms with a medium grade sand paper – around 130 grit. Anything coarser might leave scratch marks which would require additional sanding to remove. Do a finish sanding with 220 grit paper.

15. <u>Paint the parts.</u> Apply the first coat of a good exterior primer. When it is dry, the grain of the wood will be raised. Lightly sand all over with a 220 grit paper and apply the second coat of primer and allow it to dry.

Apply the finish coats of paint. The gloves are red, the boots are black, and the shorts are black,

but they can be any color. For Caucasian flesh color, use white paint with a small drop of red to approximate the skin tone. For African American, use brown with a small amount of white. It might take a little experimenting, and other colors like yellow can be added to get the desired tone.

16. <u>Final assembly.</u> When the paint dries, the whirligig can be reassembled (see step 11). Add lock washers or a drop of Loctite thread locker to the shaft on both sides for the insert and lock nuts. Readjust the arms so that they spin freely and stop in random positions. Mount the boxer outside, and observe how it reacts to the wind.

Usually whirligigs require a break-in period of a few weeks. The wood will absorb moisture from the air and expand, or it may dry out a little. During this period, further adjustment may be required. The arms may bind up and refuse to spin. If the arms bind against the body, loosen the lock nut on one side and rotate the arm out one or two turns. If there seems to be clearance on the sides, but the shaft is stuck, this may be caused by the body swelling or warping slightly and constricting the shaft. Remove the shaft and bushings and open up the hole through the body with a slightly larger drill. Sometimes final adjustments might be needed after a couple of weeks.

FIGURE 8.5

9

Creating Original Whirligigs

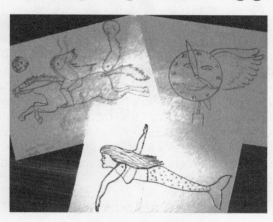

FIGURE 9.1

After you have made a whirligig or two, whether from the plans in this book or from someone else's instructions, you might consider designing and making your own originals. If you begin by following the guidelines in the previous chapters, and use relatively simple themes, there is no reason you won't succeed. The subject matter is unlimited, and the possibilities are endless. Any errors in design or construction may be easily repaired or covered up with epoxy putty and paint. Folk art doesn't have to be perfect, and often irregularities have a rustic charm. As you progress, you may experiment with different construction techniques, and with more complicated and imaginative designs.

No doubt, there is money to be made creating whirligigs. While I wouldn't tout this as a get-rich-quick scheme, there is an immense market for original, handmade works of art. As more and more so-called art is mass-produced and computer generated, there is a growing appreciation for one-of-a-kind creations. Whirligigs will always be in demand because they are a pleasure to own and watch, are colorful and fun, active and amusing, original and artistic - genuine Americana. If you invest the time, develop the skills, produce an original, quality product and price it correctly, you may find you can support yourself with a full time hobby.

For those of us who are interested in whirligigs regardless of any economic incentives, there is always a new reason to make another original. Everyone with a porch, a balcony, or a back yard should have at least one. When word gets out you are making them, everyone will want one. People who haven't realized yet that they want one should get one as a gift. In addition, since people have different tastes, there will always be a need for new designs, or improvements on old ones. It's fun to be creative, especially when there is an outlet for your creativity.

In a New England seaport town, I saw a simple silhouette whirligig of a lobster with twirling claws that was getting much attention. I know with a woodcarver's touch, it could be made much better. Just the other day a friend demanded to know when he was getting a whirligig, and of course, it must be a leprechaun swinging a shillelagh. Perhaps it might be appropriate to make a whirligig of the Headless Horseman, in tribute to Washington Irving. His black steed is charging and his hands are moving, but what is that he is holding? Is it a pumpkin, or is it his head? Moreover, how about a whirligig of a . . .?

I hope you have enjoyed reading this book. I hope by reading the book you have gained an appreciation for arm-waving whirligigs and a better understanding of their design and construction. However, most of all, I hope you have at least started to make one for yourself, or have jotted down an idea or a sketch for an awesome whirligig. If you haven't, what are you waiting for?

ACKNOWLEDGEMENTS

I am indebted to many people for their support in making this book possible. Joan Gould and Colonel Bernie O'Neil USMC gave invaluable editorial assistance. J. Richard O'Neil aided with a careful read of the manuscript. Jennifer O'Neil used her sharp eyes and good judgment in locating grammatical faux pas. Bryna Stello provided essential production guidance. Jerry O'Neil contributed with his usual in-depth technical expertise. Thanks to Julie Conway for a skilled and thorough proof read. Last, but not least, I'm grateful to my wonderful wife Martha, for her constant encouragement and patience during this time-consuming but enjoyable project.

Appendices

Sources of Supplies

Woodcarving Supplies

Craft Woods
P. O. Box 527
Timonium, MD 21094-0527
800-468-7070

Dremel
P. O. Box 1468
Racine, Wisconsin 53401

Wood Carvers Supply, Inc.
P. O. Box 7500
Englewood FL, 34295-7500
800-284-6229

Woodcraft Supply
41 Atlantic Ave.
Woburn, MA 01888
800-225-1153

Mechanical Components

The Foredom Electric Co.
16 Stony Hill Road
Bethel, CT 06810

Loctite Corporation
1001 Trout Brook Crossing
Rocky Hill, CT 06067-3910

Small Parts Inc.
13980 N. W. 58thCourt
P. O. Box 4650
Miami Lakes, FL 33014-0650
800-220-4242

The Steco Corporation
P. O. Box 2238
Little Rock, Arkansas 72203

Organizations

National Wood Carvers Association
7424 Miami Ave.
Cincinnati, OH 45243
513-561-0627
Annual membership and subscription to Chip Chats
magazine $14.00. (Highly recommended)

New England Woodcarvers, Inc.
P. O. Box 561
Lexington, MA 02420-0005
Annual membership and subscription to Newsletter
$15.00.

Museums

Henry Ford Museum & Greenfield Village
20900 Oakwood Blvd
Dearborn, Michigan 48124

Higgins Armory Museum
100 Barber Ave.
Worcester, MA 01606

Old Sturbridge Village
1 Old Sturbridge Village Road
Sturbridge, MA 01566

Shelburne Museum
U. S. Route 7
P.O. Box 10
Shelburne, VT 05482

Bibliography

Whirligigs

Bishop, Robert Charles & Patricia Coblentz, *A Gallery of American Weathervanes and Whirligigs*, 1981, Bonanza Books, New York.

Bridgewater, Alan & Gill Bridgewater, *The Wonderful World of Whirligigs and Wind Machines*, 1990, McGraw-Hill, New York.

Burda, Cindy, *Wind Toys That Spin, Sing, Twirl & Whirl,* 1999, Sterling Publishing Co.

Crepeau, Pierre, *Playing With the Wind, the Whirligig Collection of the Canadian Museum of Civilization,* 1991, Canadian Museum of Civilization.

Fitzgerald, Ken, *Weathervanes and Whirligigs,* 1967, Crown Publishing Group.

Frost, Rodney, *Whacky Toys, Whirligigs & Whatchamacallits,* 2002, Sterling Publishing Co.

Hooke, Richard, *Blowing in the Wind: How to Make Your Own Wind Powered Folk Art Figures* 1987, Down East Books.

Kilby, Janice Eaton, *By Hand: 25 Beautiful Objects to Make in the American Folk Art Tradition,* 2001, Sterling Publishing Co.

Lunde, Anders S., *Action Whirligigs: 25 Easy-to-Do Projects, 2003.*
   Easy-to-Make Whirligigs, 1982, (Highly recommended).
   Making Animated Whirligigs, 1998.
   Whimsical Whirligigs and How to Make Them, 2000, Dover Publications, Inc., 31 East 2 [nd]
      Street, Mineola, N. Y. 11501-3582.
   Whirligigs in Silhouette, 1989, K. C. Publishing Co., Kansas City.
   Whirligigs for Children Young and Old, 1992, Kraus Publications.
   More Whirligigs: Large-Scale and Animated Figures, 1985, Kraus Publishing.
   Whirligigs: Design and Construction, 1982, The Chilton Book Company.
   Whirligigs, 1986, Kraus Publications.

Pettit, Florence Harvey, *How to Make Whirligigs and Whimmy Diddles and Other American Folkcraft Objects*, 1972, Crowel, New York.

Pierce, Sharon, *Making Whirligigs and Toys,* 1985, Sterling Publishing Co.

Schoonmaker, David & Bruce Woods, *Whirligigs and Weathervanes: A Celebration of Wind Gadgets, with Dozens of Projects to Make,* 1992, Sterling, New York.

Schwarz, Renee, *Wind Chimes and Whirligigs (Kids Can Do It),* 2007, Kids Can Press.

Whiley, Jack , *How to Make Animated Whirligigs, Kids on Teeter-Totter, Carousel, and Flying Duck,* 1991.
   How to Make More Animated Whirligigs: Girl Gymnast, Ferris Wheel, Unicyclist, 1991.
   How to Make Propeller Animated Whirligigs, Penguin, Folk Rooster, Dove, Pink Flamingo, Flying Unicorn and Road Runner, 1993.
   Whirligig Book: How to Make Action Mechanical Whirligigs, 1990,
      Solipaz Publishing Co.

Uniforms and Costumes

Mollo, John & Malcolm McGreggor, *Uniforms of the American Revolution*, 1975, Blandford Press.

Vesey, Norman, *Arms and Armour,* 1972, Octopus Books .

Military Uniforms, the Splendour of the Past, 1973, Orbis Books, London.

General

Irving, Washington, *The Legend of Sleepy Hollow*

Selected Woodcarving Books

Burk, Bruce, *Game Bird Carving,* 1972, Winchester Press, New York.

Christensen, Erwin O., *Early American Wood Carving,* 1972, Dover Publications, New York.

Edlin, Herbert L., *What Wood is That?* 1969, The Viking Press, New York.

Gilley, Wendell, *The Art of Bird Carving,* 1972, Hillcrest Pulblishing, Inc. Spanish Fork, Utah.

Fractions – Inches – Millimeters Conversions

Fractions	Inches	Millimeters		Fractions	Inches	Millimeters
1/32	.03125	.794		17/32	.53125	13.494
1/16	.0625	1.588		9/16	.5625	14.288
3/32	.09375	2.381		19/32	.59375	15.081
1/8	**.125**	**3.175**		**5/8**	**.625**	**15.875**
5/32	.15625	3.969		21/32	.65625	16.669
3/16	.1875	4.762		11/16	.6875	17.462
7/32	.21875	5.556		23/32	.71875	18.256
1/4	**.25**	**6.350**		**3/4**	**.75**	**19.050**
9/32	.28125	7.144		25/32	.78125	19.844
5/16	.3125	7.938		13/16	.8125	20.638
11/32	.34375	8.731		27/32	.84375	21.431
3/8	**.375**	**9.525**		**7/8**	**.875**	**22.225**
13/32	.40625	10.319		29/32	.90625	23.019
7/16	.4375	11.112		15/16	.9375	23.812
15/32	.46875	11.906		31/32	.96875	24.606
1/2	**.5**	**12.700**		**1**	**1.000**	**25.400**

Troubleshooting Whirligigs

If problems develop with arm-waving or split-wing whirligigs that have been constructed with the techniques and components shown in this book, here are some suggestions:

If the whirligig's arms or wings won't spin:
Do a visual inspection.
> **If the arms/wings are tight against the body**, or **if one of the arms is hitting the body or base:**
>> Loosen the lock nut on one of the arms and rotate the arm out one or two turns, add a drop of thread locker, realign and retighten.

Gently turn the arms by hand if possible.
> **If there is constriction of the shaft:**
>> Remove one of the arms and slide the other arm, bushings and shaft out of the body. Open up the shaft hole in the body with a drill bit slightly larger than the existing hole.
> **If the shaft is bent:**
>> Remove one of the arms and slide the other arm and shaft out of the body. Straighten or replace the shaft.

If it's very windy, but the whirligig's arms only spin occasionally:
Check the fit of the whirligig on its pivot point.
> **If the whirligig doesn't rotate freely on the pivot point:**
>> Make sure the pivot rod or nail has clearance in the pivot hole in the whirligig body. Make sure the copper tube liner and the stainless steel ball are intact inside the pivot hole, and replace if necessary.
> **If the whirligig rotates freely on the pivot point, but the arms still only spin occasionally:**
>> Make sure the arms aren't hitting the body or base, the bushings aren't missing or binding, or the shaft isn't bent or constricted in the body. It is possible the pivot point may be located incorrectly. Consider removing the copper tube and steel ball, filling the hole with epoxy putty, and re-drilling a pivot hole in a better location or at a better angle.

If the whirligig's arms only spin when it's very windy:
Both of the arms may be too heavy or thick. Disassemble the arms and remove material evenly from both until the propeller section is about 1/8 inch thick. Remove excess material evenly from the shoulder sections. Alternatively, the propeller section may not be cut at a sharp enough angle. Remove material where possible so the blade is not facing front to back or side to side, but is closer to a 45-degree angle.

If the whirligig's arms always end up in a horizontal (inverted "v") position:
One or both of the arms are loose on the shaft. Realign the arms and tighten the lock nuts, using liquid thread locker if necessary.

If one of the whirligig's arms or wings always ends up on the bottom:
One of the arms is heavier than the other is, or has more material on its end. Remove the lower arm and determine where material may be removed. Carve or file off some material, reassemble and test. When the arms always end in random positions, prime and repaint the reworked arm, and reassemble.

INDEX

Page numbers in *italics* indicate information in illustrations.

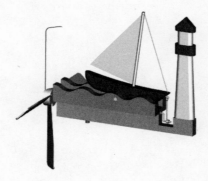

Visit us at online at www.mandmarts.com.